LIBERATION OF THE ACTOR

Liberation of the Actor

Peter Bridgmont

TEMPLE LODGE
London

First edition 1992

A catalogue record for this book is available from the British Library

ISBN 0 904693 33 3

Cover art: 'Hamlet' by E.B. Gordon.   Design: S. Gulbekian.
Author photograph: Simeon Bläsi.

Typeset by DP Photosetting, Aylesbury, Bucks
Printed and bound in Great Britain by
Billing & Sons Ltd, Worcester

To all my students,
past and present.

Acknowledgements

First of all I wish to thank my wife Barbara for her patience and suggestions, and for contributing the exercises for lyric, epic and dramatic styles of speech (Chapter 11). A special debt is owed to Maisie Jones, Principal of the Speech School, East Grinstead, for her practical support and encouragement. And finally I thank Eileen Lloyd for her valuable editorial help.

Contents

Preface

This is neither a textbook on the theatre nor a training manual for student actors. It is more in the nature of a discussion on the possible future of the theatre and the actor's contribution to that future.

Much of the material contained here comes from my book *The Spear Thrower* (now out of print). The ideas in that earlier publication have since been worked on and developed and are now presented with fresh thoughts and suggestions which I hope will prove helpful to readers.

In my experience, the drama student is directed towards character analysis and interpretation much too early in his or her training. Though accuracy and detail of character and situation are of undoubted value, there are other aspects of the theatre even more appreciated by an audience. For example, the young actor should learn that dialogue in the theatre is quite a different process to that experienced in everyday conversation. The speech should live within the audience—which does not just mean projecting the voice. In training, a sense should be developed of the speech existing free of the actor. An audience should be able to live within the dynamic of the speech as well as the moods expressed through the tones; they will then participate in the sound because the speech surrounds them.

The idea of existing in the body of the theatre must also be trained into the actor's movement. He should feel when he moves upstage that the people in the audience are drawn with him. When he moves to their right or left upon the stage, they should share this movement. Instead of simply watching the performers moving to and fro, the audience should inwardly move with them, as though they were watching dancers.

A performer's secret ambition should be that the character he or she is playing will in no way display self-resemblance—no tone, gesture, attitude or expression in voice or manner should resemble his or her own personality. I remember when working with Theatre Workshop at the Theatre Royal, Stratford, Joan Littlewood commenting that the audience always knew when a performance was a complete creation of the actor or when it relied on the actor's personality. In the first instance the audience will join you, but in the second they will somehow be disappointed.

From such ambitions came Edward Gordon Craig's hope for the actor at the beginning of this century. He believed that an individual who could experience gesture and voice as objective instruments would place the actor again as a fitting servant of the art of drama.

There is an invisible force of theatre, a stream or 'waterfall' of energy upon which the actor moves and speaks. This is what I believe the early Greeks meant when they spoke of *rhythmos*. With the increasing interest in social realism and psychology in the modern theatre, something has been lost as well as gained in the quality of acting. For instance, Sir Ralph Richardson, in an interview, spoke of the continuity of energy throughout a production—possibly our rhythmos. He likened a performance to a stone rolling down a hill. In comedy, when the drama ended, the stone came to rest in the fields below. In tragedy, it shattered. Only an actor can speak of such realities. The interviewer, I remember, was at a complete loss as to what to make of the actor's comments. Actors and actresses must become aware again of such esoteric experiences in their art.

A discussion about such ideas is part of the content of this book. What is that quality among fine artists that lifts one above the other? In the world of music the technique is often so remarkable that other, esoteric qualities are not taken into account. Those are the qualities once described to me by a musician who had the final say in the choice of artists for a season at a concert hall. 'There are those who play well,' he said, 'and those who play very well, but there are those for whom we dig deep into our pockets for their services. For they die into their music, and the music then becomes free. Also, the listener then becomes free of the artist.' Something of the same nature could exist again in the theatre.

This book attempts to remind us of aspects of acting which are being abandoned or forgotten. We should not think in terms of resurrecting the old but of creating a firm base of ideals for the theatre of the future.

Introduction

To speak of the liberation of the actor must to some seem ridiculous, for surely the actor is more liberated today than he has ever been. He or she can walk on the stage, comb their hair, take off their shoes, wash their hands. In fact, the actor can do anything at any time, and as long as it is in the realm of probability it will be acceptable to actors, producers and audience alike. We will take it for granted that all the actions are performed with skill, but to question whether today's actor is free hardly seems valid. For instance, we perform on all manner of staging, from thrust staging, to theatre-in-the-round. We perform in the streets, in rooms above pubs, in proscenium theatres and civic halls whose ceilings are adorned with full lighting equipment. There is nothing we do not do.

Freedom even extends into the acting itself. The urge to move is all that is necessary in order to carry out some action. The urge to speak is enough to justify speaking on the stage. Are we no more to be hampered by training in deportment, or in voice production as it was called? Are these but handicaps to the free expression of the artist or whoever may be attempting to act?

What we are discussing is not just the need for training but the thinking behind the work in theatre. If all our work is only as good or as advanced as our own personality or our capacity for thought or poetry, then the limits placed on the art are as circumscribed as the artist's own life experience and character.

One of the miracles of art is that a painting, a dance or a musical performance is often a world apart from the personality of the artist. He or she can go beyond themselves in their art and beyond their own personality. Indeed, one can sometimes be disappointed when meeting an artist of calibre because he seems so ordinary compared to the presentation on the stage or recital platform. Conversely, it can be equally surprising when you have witnessed a performance in a play and then discover the performer is exactly the same off-stage. In the academic world one can come across a similar contrast, of someone's immense erudition with his everyday personality. I remember talking to a specialist on a subject, telling me how disappointed he was when he met the author of the textbook which as a student he had studied and revered. Compared to the mental brilliance displayed in his book, the man seemed quite ordinary. This to me is one of the many miracles of the human being.

To speak well and to carry oneself well upon the stage may have little to do with acting but a great deal to do with consciousness. I do not recommend a straining after beautiful speech or graceful movement. What is to be recommended, however, is a study of speech and movement that shows the actor to be an authority on these matters, and this would help to justify his existence.

'O Man know thou thyself', was the ancient Greek adage. 'Know thyself and you will understand the universe'. What could they have meant by this? The actor of the past believed he must reveal through the human drama the reality from which the human sprang. Sybil Thorndike, the actress, once said that actors were expected to show 'the particular and the universal at the same time'. For instance, I once saw an actor in a play push a bottle of wine from him in such a way that we felt it to be the character's dismissal of his whole life and career. The 'particular' was pushing away a life with which he was disgusted. The actor performed both duties to perfection.

For the Greek actor, to breathe in and exhale was not only to keep all pumps going in his body; when he breathed in, he could lift himself into the realm of thought and inspiration, and when he breathed out he could expel into the air his will to perform deeds. He felt his speaking and singing came from a realm other than the everyday. Even in Elizabethan times our breathing and heartbeat was considered a reflection of the movement of the planets. It was Shakespeare who, for the first time, portrayed characters that spoke against such universal ideas. Thus Edmund, in the play *King Lear*, expresses his feelings on the matter:

This is the excellent foppery of the world, that when we are sick in fortune—often the surfeit of our own behaviour—we make guilty of our disasters the sun, the moon, and the stars; as if we were villains by necessity, fools by heavenly compulsion . . .

The miracle of today's drama is that we have the skills to show the familiar with great accuracy of observation. If only at the same time we could reveal the hidden strengths supporting our movement and speech. If we could only show that the appearance is in many respects 'unreal' and that there is an invisible reality which fires mankind. This reality can be found in philosophy, geometry and art; it can also be shown in dance and song, and in the weird and wonderful art of acting and drama. The actor is but the servant to the drama. He can display the world as he knows it but through his study and training he can reveal in his movement and speaking the world behind this world, which supports our scribblings to do with everyday life. What such words as these may fail to convey, acting can accomplish; the drama may appear normal and conventional, yet behind the actor's work the true human spirit caught in the tapestry of everyday life may begin to be revealed. The artist used to be called 'the messenger of the gods'. The messenger may occasionally forget his place and think his task is to be a god, and this can look very strange and foolish but, all the same, as with all artists, the position of being a messenger is one of high honour. It was after all the most important role in the ancient Greek drama. Can once again the art of the messenger bring new visions to the people, by his power of description and dramatization? Let us hope so.

CHAPTER 1
Where is the Actor?

In the 1850s, acting was turning in on itself; like the contemporary popular novel, it was beginning to depict situations and conversations in an increasingly true-to-life manner. The excitement engendered in the theatre was intense when actors, influenced by Edmund Keen, showed characters such as Shylock or Richard III reacting to their circumstances in a way familiar to the audience in their everyday life.

One could imagine the sense of immediacy this form of acting brought about, and Konstantin Stanislavsky amongst many others began to devote serious study to it. One of the first questions was: where is the actor during this process? Putting it another way: where is the individual during the action? Is he part of the action, or is he separate from it, pretending to be concerned with the situation but really only 'play-acting'? Or is his own personality so deeply involved in the enactment of the character in the story or plot that a kind of reality is brought to the fictional situation?

This question still needs to be resolved. Its answer will surely provide some idea of where we are at present in the history of drama, and where our direction lies in looking towards the future.

Where was the actor in the ancient Greek theatre? We know of course that physically he was hidden behind his mask, standing in his high boots (cothurnus), facing a large semicircle of spectators, his back to the sea or plains, his head and thoughts in the blue sky above him, and his feet stepping out the choreographed rhythmical dance on the circle of stone. But where was he, the actor? Was he with his singing and chanting and his stepping in his thick-soled boots while moving his head this way and that, directing the fixed expression of his mask? During the play he often performed

4

two or three characters, each with the physical limitations of the cothurnus, costume, mask and the choreography, song and speech.

The answer to this question could be in a fresco now in the Museo Archeologico Nazionale, Naples. It shows a weary actor resting after a performance, while a woman kneels before the mask with adoration, her back to the actor. I think for some of us this painting is an indication of where the actor of ancient times thought he should be. Nevertheless, the sun, sky, and architecture holding the spectators with the sense of festival must have put the performers in a state of intense excitement. His theatre was open, not closed in with a roof over his head. The actor could breathe in such a theatre. It was the home of dramatic speaking.

Historians of drama tell us that acting descended into comedy and mime, and that a style developed which was the precursor of naturalistic acting. Comedy depicts events set in familiar surroundings in which fantastic happenings can occur. This is the comic polarity. Even in ancient times it was exploits in the kitchen and disasters in the pantry. The comic style speaks to us of ourselves and our behaviour, and this is what makes us laugh. We cannot laugh at the unknown or the unfamiliar; only when situations descend into the familiar can we laugh at them.

Let us now hasten down the centuries to the era of the pageant dramas and the guild plays. The amateur performers with their childlike imagination portrayed Noah, Caesar, Joseph, Herod, the Devil, in the streets, on movable wagons. They captured the people's imagination by bringing these biblical characters to life. The actor's mental pictures became actualities for the audience. We can thus picture how what we call a natural talent for acting began to develop.

Rapidly the spoken word took over from the scenic action of the guild plays. The characters 'deepened', expressing more and more their inner feelings, to the increasing interest of the audience. Finally, as we know, a theatre was built in London for the purpose of presenting plays. The Elizabethan actor was in his own home at last, the centre of his world. With his lungs, lips, tongue and palate he delivered into the air the passions, thoughts and decisions of his characters. How did he hold an audience spellbound in that theatre for two to three hours, performing

5

most complicated dramas of poetic thought? With what power did he hold them? Today, in our soft seats, we can dream our way through a play.

We know that the bold gestures of the Elizabethan actor sprang from tradition (for example, the gesture of beating the hand with the fist to make a point), and of course all gestures and mimes could be learnt. Yet gesture was not enough. Was attention consistently commanded by the way of speaking? I believe the speaking at that time, with those plays and in that theatre, must have been paramount as the instrument of drama. It could not have been roaring, for Hamlet is very critical of such speaking on the stage. The actor's speech commanded his space and held the audience still and silent, and no doubt he used the emphatic and effective style of the story-teller and the epic speaker. I feel sure that those trained in 'eloquence' in the sixteenth century were well aware of this epic-speaking style and transferred it to the art of acting, as a firm basis for speaking in the theatre. This style of speaking we will come back to later in the book.

With the appearance of the proscenium arch at the end of the sixteenth century, the actor was banished from the platform within the circle of the audience and the gallery; his acting area was now behind the arch, where he joined the scenery behind the curtain. This change of position of the actor dimly heralded the cinema screen and eventually the television box.

The actor was no more the centre of his world, and this had its consequences. Also, his outer world had closed in upon him. In Greece the actor had the sun, the air, the sea and sky where the gods lived, those same gods that participated in his dance and dithyrambs and were the substance of drama. Even in Elizabethan theatre daylight played an essential part. One can imagine that when the theatre finally closed its eyes and roofed itself in, the actor, under such conditions, began to feel he must generate more energy from himself as he could not receive it from without. Before, life had approached him from the periphery, but now he had to urge himself outwards from the centre. For the first time, his own personality had a part to play in his art. A new enjoyment came into his acting—not from the inspiration of the gods or even through the support of religion, as in the pageant drama of the Middle Ages, but from an inner sense of creating out of himself.

The actor had to assert himself. He had to radiate out into the auditorium. His lighting glared from the ground row of floats (a system of floating wicks in oil). The spectator was a dark hole before him and he a shadow of his former self upon a gloomy platform. He was forced to project himself across to the audience through the stage archway. This contracting experience of scenery and subdued light must have produced in him a sensation quite opposite to that experienced by his colleagues at the Globe Theatre.

The projecting, thrusting style of acting which appeared from these changed circumstances led to a highly dramatic style of performance and what we know now as the 'star' system. Garrick, Kean and Macready, leading actors of the late eighteenth and early nineteenth centuries, shone with an energetic brilliance. As this energy waned later in the nineteenth century, a furthering of the contracting process turned into a seeming virtue and naturalism came fully into its own.

This very brief historical setting for the actor is only to remind us that there are qualities in dramatic acting which are being lost for the sake of a process. The acting of today in all its excellence, invention and detail is only part of a process; the other part I will discuss in the course of this book. We will now consider theatre in the twentieth century.

The Modern Theatre: Looking to the Future

From the sixteenth century until the beginning of this century, theatre remained in the picture-frame of the proscenium. This set the actor firmly into a world of action that was surrounded by scenery which pinned him like a butterfly into a painted realism. Increasingly the drama tended to be made up of characters struggling with situations near enough to everyday reality for the audience to be able to relate to them. Interest was directed more towards how the characters dealt with their problems of love and hate, and murder and betrayal, and so forth, and less towards the poetic soul of the human being. Ancient drama depicted the human being as an essential being within himself, with his own distinctive laws, beliefs and moral sense, challenging the events that came to meet him. His fate lay in the hands of the gods, or was determined by the planets in the heavens. But throughout the past 300 years mankind has come to look on himself as quite separate from the world, battling with its problems on equal terms. As a result, the essence of drama has become the portrayal of the human being confined only to the narrow limits of survival and personal destiny.

What we witness now on the stage, in the films, and so on, is but a continuation of that contracting process; drama is pressed into a square frame of the world, and limited to the framing of the proscenium. The personal destiny of the protagonist now merely depends on his or her behaviour in a situation. Even the situation becomes 'absurd', as Camus would describe it, and we are left with ourselves as no more than reacting human substance.

At the beginning of this century, many streams of artistic thought repulsed the evolving naturalistic drama, particularly in Germany. All that we have left of this time is Konstantin Stanislavsky, who was not considered more important than many others working in different directions. Impressionism, primitivism, abstractionism, ecstatic acting, alienation, epic theatre are but a few theatrical experiments in the early days of this century. Without doubt the strongest force was the impressionistic theatre, represented (if one has to pigeonhole) by the theatre designer and director Edward Gordon Craig and the Swiss scenery artist Adolphe Appia, to name but two.

Stanislavsky clarified what was the finalising of a long historical process which arrived at the beginning of the twentieth century, appearing to be new. Naturalism was like Darwin's theory of the evolution of species—there was something inevitable about it. But in Germany there was a spirit of enterprise, invention and idealism which sprang from the human being alone and sought to break the contracting frame which squeezed the theatre into the shape we know.

Many artists at that time, in painting, music, dance, and drama were not part of an inevitable process but spoke, acted, designed and composed out of themselves. They created in such a way that one wonders from where their ideas came. I am continually amazed at Craig's writings. All his ideas were new, self-created, not reflections of the old, even though he came from the traditional theatre of England. His mother, Ellen Terry, was considered the greatest actress of her time. She performed at the Lyceum Theatre, London, with Henry Irving, who was considered the greatest actor of his time. So Craig was born into a famous family of artists and moved among the finest actors of his time, yet he developed his own thoughts on theatre that had little to do with any of theirs.

He started with the scenery. In his day 'realism' was all the rage. A palace on the stage had to look like a palace, and a garden like a garden, although much of the scenery was painted on flats with shadows and perspective. Young Craig, dissatisfied with this, presented his own productions. First he stripped the stage bare and removed the pelmet from the proscenium arch, then, using one or two rostrums and a large cyclorama, he bathed the stage in sunlight. Thus he created for the actor a 'place'. This 'place' challenged the new naturalistic actor.

Imagine a large acting area of pale wooden boards. On the stage stand towering screens in pale terracotta. Up-stage, behind us, is a horizon with the light blue sky rising to white above us. A rostrum runs the length of the base of the sky. There is apparently no off-stage, only space going on and on. You walk to the centre of the stage, or stumble on, or shuffle on, or pace on, or drift on, or sidle on, or bounce on, but you are well aware that you have actually walked onto a 'stage'.

The space tells you where you are standing: at the side, off-centre, up-stage, down-stage. Wherever you are, the stage informs you of your position. As a modern actor, you may feel uncertain that you are being 'within yourself' or, as they have instructed you so often, are 'projecting from your centre'. You seem diminutive. If you try to radiate from your centre, it is as though the space laughs at you as you puff yourself up. The space, the sky, the light and the air wait for you; the theatre is waiting for you to join it in the art of drama.

Silence reigns, stillness waits. You pace across the stage and turn on your heel. Silence remains, stillness yawns. A flicker of expression contorts your face. Silence stares, stillness laughs. You shove your hands in your pockets. You kick your feet. You begin to think you are establishing yourself in this area. You are not; you are behaving like someone who is off-stage. You pick your teeth

9

for a moment, run your hand through your hair, lift an eyebrow, saunter, whistle and then stand. Silence reigns, stillness waits. A burst of energy, you leap, you shout, you thrust out your arm. 'Once more unto the breach dear friends, once more.' Your voice cuts through the space, and the silence immediately moves in and heals the wound. You are radiating from your centre, projecting, declaiming—a few 'shadow' gestures (see pp. 15 and 36) and you stand panting, unsure and despondent. The theatre seems to ignore you, and yet it seems to expect something—something else?

Could it be that, instead of standing in the space and trying to fill it from your centre, you could feel energy coming towards you from the periphery of the stage, as though the impulse to move, to think, to feel, came from outside oneself? Could those ideas, motivations (or whatever names you wish to give to that 'will to act') approach from another world? Picture this other world as the realm of the imagination. You call in thoughts; when you wish to speak, you call in breath. The words you speak are approaching from the world of thought, that is, in a way, off-stage. So your movements and speaking are supported from outside—you live in a world of buoyancy.

Gordon Craig prepared a place for such feelings and such acting, which stood as a personal challenge to all that was flooding into the twentieth century from the three previous centuries.

EXERCISE: UNDERWATER MIME

To develop a feeling for the periphery, we should do the following 'underwater mime'. We stand like seaweed under the water, floating gently with the current. As we imagine the sea moves, so we, as seaweed move. The response of the seaweed reveals the motion of the sea. If it is turbulent, the seaweed's response will show it. If it is calm, the seaweed will drift calmly. We can make any list of emotions and situations, such as those opposite, or extend the exercise by using a sequence from a scene in a play. The actor/dancer always feels that he is responding to a larger activity around him. ▶

Storm approaching—apprehension fear
Storm stronger—anger
Calm water (seaweed hanging in space)—stillness, tranquillity
Swirling currents keep striking—suddenness
Underwater swells—danger looms
Turbulent water—trouble and strife
Swift underwater currents—tension
Splashing water—jollity
Water drains away—death
Sudden cold patches of water—anxiety
Very warm water—generosity
Very cold water—bitterness
Dark water—sense of loss

The sea, tranquil before an approaching storm, will gradually move till eventually the seaweed appears to be gesticulating as though in a rage. But it is the sea that is turbulent, while under the surface it is the seaweed that shows it. This exercise gradually expands the actors' and actresses' awareness to an area outside themselves, enveloping the mood on the stage and in the whole theatre. Not only do the actor's instincts develop to include the space around, but he may then consider that much of what we think and feel approaches us from the universe, as the Greek believed in his theatre. This door can open, to allow the actor the freedom to live entirely in the body of the theatre.

CHAPTER 2
Story-telling, Mime and Gesture: The Foundation

Drama is story-telling. The narrator's function has gradually passed to the actor. The story is revealed through activity, and through the duologue between performers.

All actors should at some time speak in the epic style, enunciating the consonants as though to form the speech into shapes. The listener inwardly receives the speech form which stirs the inner image-making capacity we all possess.

The imagination required by the epic speaker and the listener is formed out of the *will* of the speaker and the listener. The will of the speaker appears in the formation of the consonants; this can lead to a certain emphatic style, which is part of story-telling and should lie behind all speaking for the stage. We know that an effective quality of speaking is very much part of the actor's art. When you wish to be fully understood by the listener, you can speak in a slow, emphatic, carefully enunciated manner, so that the attention of the listener is fully concentrated on your words. Coleridge, in his *Ancient Mariner*, tells how the Mariner, when wishing to relate his story to the Bridegroom, 'holds him with his glittering eye'. This is all part of story-telling and of play-acting.

An Exercise in Story-telling

It is possible to find a gesture in each single word. To illustrate this, mime a story while a speaker reads it, one word at a time, as though each word is in itself a total experience. Don't allow a single word to be skipped over, not even such prepositions as 'in', 'at', 'to', nor adverbs such as 'hastily' or 'grudgingly'. The beginning is slow but each word gradually becomes full of meaning and significance.

My own experience after carefully miming every single word in this way has been to discover just how much I had previously overlooked, both in images and expressions, at the first reading.

After the performer has mimed and moved a few sentences, he should take his turn to read them. He will then be able to relive the words he mimed and even danced in his speaking. This introduces the actor to a style for speaking epic and narration, and also to the idea that the whole basis for his means of expression in speech must rest securely on the firm foundation of the fully spoken word.

Part of a Chinese story to be spoken in epic style and each word mimed by the actor: 'Han Ma Liang and the Magic Paintbrush'. One day he was walking through the nearby town with a bundle of firewood on his back when he saw a teacher painting a picture in a private school. Scarcely thinking what he did, Liang walked inside and asked the teacher if he would give him a brush, as he so much wanted to paint. The man looked in astonishment at the bundle of rags from which the request had come.

'What a cheek!' he said. 'Do you think the refined art of painting is meant for vagabonds and beggars? Get out of my school and back to your work.' He took up his brush once more and tried to forget the interruption, while Liang walked disconsolately away.

He did not give up hope. If he could not work with the correct materials he would practise with whatever came to hand. After a long day on the mountainside gathering enormous bundles of sticks, he would set his burden down for a while and look for a flat rock. On it he would draw pictures with a flint—landscapes, beasts and birds. When he went down to the river to fish, he would spend the last hour tracing outlines in the sunbaked mud with a sharp stick. At home he covered the walls of his cave with drawings of the scenes he had witnessed during the day, so that the other villagers would stare in surprise and say the pictures seemed to be alive, they were so full of expression. Liang was held back by only one thing—he still needed a brush.

13

(It may be an idea to do this exercise again later, after getting further into this book.)

Mime

In mime we don't have the actual object itself; we shape it into existence out of the otherwise empty space. A cup is revealed by the way the hand holds the cup. A table is revealed by the way we slide our hands across the space, when laying the cloth. It is the space between the performer's hands that reveals the object. Thus, when we describe a table, a chair, or a door, we 'stroke' the object into existence.

Because he has to describe a story, like the one about the magic paintbrush, in a kind of sign language, word by word, the actor begins to sense what it is to shape and handle space, to see space as possessing a plasticity of its own.

This sense for shaping the space within the gesture enlivens his movements. More fundamentally, it prepares him for carrying the same approach over into his speaking. We shall come to this later.

EXERCISES TO DEVELOP A SENSE FOR HANDLING SPACE

Disciplined imagination is not mere pedantic correctness. Subjects for mimes can include such things as:

Clay modelling, creating pots, dishes, etc.
An artist painting with a long paintbrush, working on a canvas at a distance from him.
Opening leaves of a table, laying a cloth, setting candles on the table, lighting them.
'The house of doors'—moving through a house into various sized rooms, from banqueting hall to larder, from larder to a large staircase, and then to a narrow corridor.

Visible and Invisible Gesture

Consider the situation when you slowly raise an arm. Now, reflect on this possibility: that you can experience the action of raising an arm without actually raising it. The action is there, but it has become your decision whether you make the gesture visible by allowing the arm to follow the impulse to lift it.

Thus, we may inwardly wish to reach for a plate of food but outwardly restrain ourselves from doing it. The invisible gesture was there. We just did not *show* it. This simple idea is the *first principle in acting*.

The actor must experience his gestures inwardly. What he chooses to show visibly is his artistic decision. Let us imagine this so-called inward or invisible gesture to be not just inward but to surround us outwardly. It is larger than us, and most certainly more dynamic and living than anything we can *show* physically.

There is a tendency at present to copy only the slight and stunted indications of expression that are visible in behaviour, and to regard these as our total medium of expression in the art of acting. If, however, we can include a sense of the invisible gesture in our preparations at least, we will feel free to choose a style of expression far beyond the representation of conventional behaviour.

Shadow Gesture

Rudolf Laban spoke of the 'sickness of the age', from his point of view, as being the 'shadow gesture'. This is the incomplete gesture: those vague hand movements, twitches or, in his terminology, flicks and dabs, copied so assiduously by the actors of today in order to appear natural. What, strictly speaking, is a complete gesture? Remember that when we speak of gesture we not only speak of the 'appearance' of the gesture physically, but also the towering soul gesture which surrounds its physical manifestation, the hidden soul gesture. Much more of our inner life can be revealed by movement and speaking than is allowed by our conventional habit. Therefore, we have 'iceberg' acting or behaviour, where more lies below the surface than we want to show.

Holding up a mirror to the life of today, we often only hint at depths of feeling seething under the surface of the visible behaviour. If characters were instead to express their innermost thoughts and feelings on the stage, they would burst into a mode of behaviour quite unacceptable to current fashions.

Often in productions of *King Lear* one has been more impressed by the way in which the actor has *avoided* playing the King than by anything positive in the interpretation!

Imagine what activity of soul there is in all of us, unrevealed to ourselves or others! In art we must endeavour to find a form that can reveal more truly what lies behind human behaviour.

Revealing the Real Gesture

The actor needs to dance the gesture. This expanding process begins to reveal the nature of the *real* gesture behind its naturalistic appearance. We will return to this frequently later.

Within the drama, the actor may only wish to express apprehensiveness in the smallest possible way—by playing with a pencil, for instance. But having experienced something much *larger* beforehand, in connection with this gesture, something immeasurable is added to the miming of everyday actions.

In the past, actors sought to show as much as was possible of the invisible gesture. Hence, the whole style of acting was vastly different to what it is today.

How much the actor wishes to show of the invisible gesture is his decision; but he must always be stimulated by his previous experience of the larger gesture.

Mime gesture alone can often be inhibiting, but that transparent instrument of human expression, the human voice, can reveal the magnitude of his invisible activity when he speaks. We will return to the subject of gesture in speaking later in this book.

* * * * *

16

In the past, the cinema copied the theatre, which was comic. Later, the theatre copied the cinema—and that has been tragic.

Living in Experiences

A feeling for character and inner mood can be experienced by taking up attitudes with the body.

Look forward with concentration. Next, while still looking forward, tip the head slightly down so that you have to peer from beneath your eyebrows. Then tip the head back slightly, as though looking down your nose. You will feel very different in each attitude. Each position should give you a feeling for the invisible gesture that would create such a posture.

Again, turn your feet inward, then outward. Each position can arouse within you a feeling for a character that would stand in such a way.

Every posture, every attitude, can hint at the hidden gesture and character. The actor can become like the musician who can on the one hand hear a tone in his imagination and then play it, or on the other hand play a tone first and then evoke an experience from the tone. *The ability to live in experiences like this is the second principle of the actor.*

Bringing the two principles together, we create a sequence of improvised movements. We can start with a series of sharp incisive gestures. We sense the mood they evoke in us. Then we judge what the next movement could be—perhaps a slow gliding sequence. Experiencing this in turn leads us to choose another gesture; and from that gesture another and so on. The actor is then living in two sorts of experiences, one sort stimulated by the physical action, the other by the invisible gesture.

Developing the sense for movement in this way would mean that in rehearsal a series of judgements dictated by this sense would run alongside the actor's attempt to convey the action of the character by means of naturalistic gesture. So, in the play, he may have to search hurriedly through some papers on a desk, open and close drawers, stop to think, cross the stage to a cabinet, slowly open a drawer, then shut it suddenly in exasperation. At least half his concentration is focused on sensing the dynamic of each gesture. This is the secret side of acting, the musicality of acting, the hidden harmony of the work.

In this way, the appearance of events on the stage is only part of the actor's work. Beyond would be a sense of form that, though invisible, creates power, a quality vital to the theatre, the quality that creates the mystery in acting, a quality only to be fully appreciated through experience. We have lost this. *Only the actor can find it again.*

On holiday, we may perhaps indulge in a favourite sport—say skiing, climbing, wind-surfing, or maybe just walking. By physical effort we come to an experience we personally enjoy. On the other hand, our expenditure of physical effort may be slight, and experience attained by an inward activity—observation of some kind, say bird watching, painting, reading, visiting places of interest, or just sitting on the seashore. Little or no physical activity is involved, but much inner activity is aroused.

This illustrates that one experience can be stimulated by outward physical effort, another by little physical effort. The actor must be able to find both sorts of experience, not only in his own movements and the tone of his voice, but also by living in imagined experiences which only appear in actions later.

Gymnastics often involve perfect balance between the two. Throwing a spear or a discus in turn arouses a feeling for weight and of flight. This experience later improves our throwing, developing a sense of throwing *before* we throw. (We shall come to this again in the next chapter.)

This process—first experience, later creative work—is the process on which the art of acting rests. We should sense these two approaches to experience and call upon them in everything we do to lift the art of acting out of the pit of naturalism into the realm of real experience.

Some Exercises

ATTITUDES TO EXPRESS

To get a sense for living, invisible gesture we can take a list of suggested moods and attitudes.

First we express an attitude in a naturalistic way. For ▶

---

example, taking 'apprehensive', we may squeeze our hands together, or scratch our chin, and so on. Usually, our action will be taken from our memory of our own experience of our own movements.

Now we turn to opening the gesture out, to expanding it further, out into space, by dancing the gesture. In doing this, we are *reaching out for the invisible gesture*—and gaining awareness of the poverty of naturalistic appearance compared with true expression.

List of attitudes

angry	doubting	miserable
anguished	eager	miserly
anxious	encouraging	mocking
apprehensive	enthusiastic	moody
astonished	envious	peaceful
awed	exasperated	pensive
awkward	fanatical	pettish
belligerant	fearful	petulent
benevolent	feckless	pompous
boisterous	fierce	powerful
bombastic	forlorn	proud
bountiful	frantic	prudish
careful	fretful	purposeful
censorious	frenzied	quaint
conceited	friendly	sanguine
concerned	garrulous	saucy
confident	generous	savage
confiding	gentle	sentimental
confused	glamorous	sinister
considerate	gloomy	sulky
contentious	grand	suspicious
courageous	longing	vague
cunning	ludicrous	vain
daunted	magnanimous	vainglorious
deliberate	malevolent	vehement
despairing	malicious	vengeful
desperate	maudlin	yearning
despondent	melodramatic	zealous

INVISIBLE GESTURE MADE VISIBLE

SECRET SELVES—AN ENTERTAINMENT

We see before us two men seated at a table. On the table is a chess set, and they are about to play. Behind each there stands a figure resembling them but more colourfully attired.

The two men gaze at the board. The game is in progress and has reached tension point. All four characters gaze at the board intently. The seated figure on the left begins to fidget with his right hand and purse his lips. The figure behind him, his secret self, expands into a posture of triumph. The player shoots out his hand, slowly raises a chess piece and then, with infinite care, sets the piece down in a new position. The seated player on the right fingers his lip in deep thought. His secret self slowly contracts in fear, ducks under its own arm and peers out. Tentatively it moves forward slowly, then hops back but after a moment moves forward again. These large movements are reflected in the tiny hesitant gesture of the seated player's hand. Finally a piece is moved.

The left-hand player's secret self curls itself into contortions of doubt. The seated partner pinches his nose thoughtfully and slowly moves a piece. Our partner on the right runs his hand through his hair with a certain vigour and then presses his fingers together. His secret self performs a dance of delight and hope. Then he creeps towards his visible self, slips his arm under the arm of the seated man and together they thrust a piece into a new position. The left-hand partner sits absolutely still but his secret self collapses in despair and so on. The mime progresses until with a whisper of 'checkmate' one of the two secret selves is struck down by the other. The two men slowly rise and with a few muttered pleasantries such as 'a good game' 'very pleasant' leave their secret selves in a transfixed stranglehold upon each other.

A SENSE OF SPACE

FROM WILLIAM SAROYAN'S *THE CAVE DWELLERS*, ACT 1, SCENE 1

A series of explosions, as buildings in the area are demolished. A girl runs into the theatre and meets the boxer, Duke.

GIRL. For the love of God, what was that?

DUKE. All right now. It's only the wreckers. They're knocking down the rotten old buildings.

GIRL. Oh, I didn't know where to run. Where am I?

DUKE. This is an old theatre. Here, I'll show you. This is the stage. There's the orchestra pit, out there's the auditorium, up there's the balcony. Can you see?

GIRL. Yes, now I can see all right. I've never seen a theatre from the stage before. It makes me feel—well, kind of proud, I guess. I don't know why, but it does. Well, I guess I'd better go now. Thanks very much.

DUKE. That's all right.

GIRL. Of course, I'd much rather stay. Can I?

DUKE. Here? No, this place is for us.

A description of the inner movement of the performers

In the tranquil pool of silence, an explosion sends a quiver through the theatre. Again the air is disturbed by a sudden explosion; now a door opens, a figure flies into the space, the movement of the actress again disturbs the space. She is lost in space, her inner space is fragmented, the performer experiences her disturbed inner space, and using this

21

experience she can flutter her words out into the bowl of the theatre, her words shaped in such a way as to recreate within the listener the flutter of fear. The Duke speaks holding the space steady with full, rounded consonants, thoughtful and weighty, calming the girl and soothing the listeners as well. She reacts to his tone and restrains her excitement. This is expressed through the following line, as between them they begin to confine the space to normal proportions: 'Oh, I didn't know where to run . . .' She withdraws into herself. Now with the awareness of the theatre as a building, she begins to expand quite consciously into the shape of the theatre. This activity becomes audible in her line 'Where am I?'

The Duke, familiar with the space he has found, leads her from the stage to the orchestra pit, right up to the gallery, again gestures helping, but the voice encircling the auditorium so that his experience of the space expanding is shared with the audience as a reality. Now she also shares the experience, and with it comes an emotional feeling of pride. Having reached this level, the actress begins inwardly to contract until she feels she has reached the right level for the line, 'Well, I guess I'd better go now'. With his line 'That's all right', he brings her down to earth. She is now small, the space is large; she begins to go, then turns and reaches out into the space, that has become a gulf between them, stepping through the line to reach him across the stage, 'Of course, I'd much rather stay. Can I?' The Duke, amazed, exclaims, 'Here?' then pushes her back with 'No, this place is for us.'

CHAPTER 3
The Body as Instrument

I would like to return to the question in Chapter 1, 'Where am *I* when I am acting?' In that chapter I was standing on the stage, in a place created by Gordon Craig, a place that he hoped would inspire the actor. Let me emphasize at this point that this is not meant to be a textbook on how to act. We will assume that you have the innate ability to act. We need to consider two impediments that may stand in the way of our acting. The first is something in our movement or speaking which may not allow us to experience acting. The second is something in ourselves, which may not allow us freely to act out of our imagination without also dragging the personal self into the picture. Therefore let us speak of means of liberating the actor's movement and speech in such a way as to equip him for his task, without once speaking of character or interpretation.

The Sense of Body Weight: A Paradox

Gymnastics gives us the chance to sense our body weight, so that we feel free from the body and yet aware of it as an instrument.

Feeling free of it comes by replacing tension with weight. An actor plagued by tension won't be able to extend himself, either through movement or through speech. Working to replace tension with a feeling of weight relaxes the muscles, enabling a greater sense of release in speaking and in gesture.

Raising an arm, turning a wrist, moving a leg, with a feeling of relaxed weight, allows the movement to be objectified. Try raising an arm, but looking at it as though it belonged to someone else. Watch the hand spread out or gently clench into a fist, but as though you stood amazed at the activity, it being something apart from yourself; then you will sense the real benefit of this awareness of weight. Of course, one is not thinking of weight as dragging or burdensome, as though one were weary or devoid of energy. What is needed is a balanced sense of weight which hovers between the pull of gravity and the natural erectness of the human being.

This objectifying of movement can be carried over into speaking. Just as we can move an arm and observe it in action, so we can speak and observe the sounds. Again, the sense of weight in the body allows us to stand balanced and at ease, so that our speech floats away from us into the surrounding air.

Tension not only hinders movement and speech but also prevents us freeing ourselves from our personal characteristics. Tension in an actor often makes his own personality obtrude too much. Releasing this tension allows something fresh and imaginative to break through.

The sense of weight can, paradoxically, lead us to experience extremes of lightness. The body can travel and weave with exceptional ease when a feeling of weight is introduced into the movement. This is how a large person can be light on his feet, yet a thin dancer or actor who is tense can fail to convey the experience of lightness and freedom.

An Exercise in Experiencing Our Body Weight

Let us sense our own weight. We will use the familiar routine of lying on the floor, on our backs, and then relaxing every part of the body until the weight seems to press into the floor. Imagine that we are trying to leave an imprint in the sand. Concentrate on breathing out more than breathing in. Here we have 'dead weight'. This 'dead weight' can lead to a belief that where my weight is there am I. A sense of weight when standing or moving on the stage will always create an impression of 'presence'. You do not have to establish yourself beyond that, to begin with; with a sense of weight you have 'arrived'. If we feel when we move or gesture that we shift our weight, the sense of effortless 'presence' is maintained. With such a sense of weight we already may be able

24

to meet Gordon Craig's scenery with some semblance of dignity. To experience this weight further, from a lying position we push ourselves up until we are standing. I say advisedly 'push oneself up' in order that we have to think how we will turn our body to push with the knee and the elbow so as to bring the body upright and so forth. This sort of exercise is not new, but for the actor it can introduce him to the levers he works with, which for him have to become a means of expression. To think through the process of pushing oneself up to a standing position makes us aware of the most physical part of us, the strange structure of bones, muscle, joints, limbs, trunk and so on.

Pictures of Passion

Continuing from the previous exercise, that is, experiencing movement but without the motive for it, we can assume physical postures—like puppets—that depict strong feelings or emotions. Each posture represents the 'picture' of an emotion, such as rage, horror, apprehension, and so forth. We set the limbs in positions which we think express it, as though we were the hieroglyphs of passion. As you hold, say, an 'imploring' gesture, try to experience the gesture as though it can tell you about itself.

The purpose of this childlike play is to awaken a sense for gesture. For the actor's art exists between the motive for the gesture and the experience from it meeting the motive. Not only is the reason for his actions important, but also that the action itself influences the actor. Acting a character during rehearsal tells us a great deal about it, and too much talk of interpretation can lose for the actor his natural instinct to find understanding out of his own gestures.

This sense of 'body articulation', and the 'shift of weight' and 'sense of balance' is not only to be experienced in heavy gestures. Psychologically, if the weight is not behind the movement then the intention in any action is weak and does not give strength or purpose to it. This one can see in everyday activity, in what Rudolf Laban calls 'shadow movements', but gesture has to be made conscious by the actor for his movement to be effective and, as we say, 'carry weight'. Therefore, as we walk on-stage, each step we take is a commitment towards the next movement. Similarly, in ancient Greek gymnastics, each step or stride taken was a training in total commitment, towards winning the race. For the actor such a sense of movement holds the attention of the audience, they sense his inner purpose.

Gymnastics

The ancient Greeks spoke of two essentials for the actor: first, courage, and second, a sense of doing the right thing immediately and instinctively. This latter quality was awakened by their gymnastic training. Perhaps we can describe this facility as unconscious co-ordination. If we are stamping and clapping, there is no time to think, although we often try to do so, but the experience of this rhythmic dancing can indicate that our bodily movement possesses a natural 'wit'. In Elizabethan times the word 'wit' referred to the physical adaptability of a character, such as could be applied to the 'witty' Morris dancing of a comedian of that time, Ned Tarleton. Such bodily wit should be a natural capacity of an actor. However, it is a talent that can be discovered and enlivened, for it is this quality which permits one to 'do the right thing at the right time'. It is as if one can have feelings, make decisions, sense the rightness or inappropriateness of a situation, in fact develop a kind of sense which can grasp situations with the sure decision of a trained athlete. It is this very same quality which moves our limbs into gestures and our speech into form. One could almost speak of another intelligence, quicker than thought, that decides and acts.

Five Gymnastic Activities

Running, leaping, discus throwing, spear (javelin) throwing and wrestling—these five gymnastic activities have the balance we had been discussing earlier. They introduce the actor to a sense of planes and directions of movement reaching into space beyond his physical gesture. They are perfectly designed to create inner and outer experiences that mutually support each other.

Running

Imagine a purpose for running. We may be running *from* something as though the runner was impelled to run; running *to* something, as though strongly attracted towards an object; or simply running for the enjoyment of it.

When we run, we feel in the upper part of our body a sense of buoyancy, as though we were flying. The Greek athletes used to run with both arms outstretched before them, in order to enhance this sense of flight. For the actor, running is an essential part of the training in order for him to experience the interplay between the upward surge of power in the legs and the supportive sense of buoyancy in the breathing area. The actor learns to become the mediator between these two experiences of air and earth.

Together with these experiences of above and below we can add the direction of the runner, when we urge ourselves forward as though goaded from behind or succumb to that which attracts us, as though pulled from the front, i.e. our need to reach the winning line. So in running these directions are united to place the actor inwardly and outwardly in the right spirit for moving and speaking.

Leaping

In leaping the athlete or performer makes a decision to do something from his own volition. We are running, trying to balance between heaven and earth, so to speak. A situation comes to meet us, some kind of obstacle—the will of the runner has to adapt to what comes towards him. He adjusts his stepping and then pushes against the earth, as a personal decision to leap the barrier. Often the performer can shout 'now', or 'go', so that movement and speech come together to give him the sense of decision. The leap itself need not be too impressive, but the *intention* can be acted out strongly to reach the right mood. This exercise helps us to experience the different dynamics in 'travelling'—slow or sustained to quick and light, the heavy swagger or the tentative approach, and so forth.

27

Discus throwing

Discus throwing releases energy into an expanding horizon, and develops the ability to handle situations outside oneself.

These two qualities arise from actually doing the exercises and gradually—though initially some 'classroom' discussion may be necessary—the exercise itself becomes the teacher.

First, the weight of the discus swings in the hand at the periphery of the body, thus pulling away as we turn. It is only because we do not release our fingertips that we retain it.

We have the impression that we are becoming stretched as we turn, stretched by the discus. Having first folded up, so to speak, into darkness, our body twisted backwards and our head down, we unwind, the discus in our hand, moving in a spiral until we are stretched forward. Then comes the great secret; that is, to *release* the discus, not throw it, not twist it, flick it, or in any way give it a final 'push'. The psychological art is to release it so that the discus spins in a clean, climbing flight. So, from our centre in a crouched position, we expand to the limits of our physical periphery and the discus flies out of our hand.

After it has been released from our hand we must watch it in flight, following its journey with our eye. This feeling of unwinding ourselves, of extending out of a spiral into flight and the sense of expanding out to the horizon provides the actor with the experience of the outer activity that must accompany all his gestures. As he moves upon the acting area he must feel that his position upon the stage effects the space of the whole theatre. As he moves up-stage he can feel how he expands the whole theatre space, as he moves downstage how he surrounds and concentrates the space. As he moves to right or left he can feel how he re-adapts the total space of the building to his position. Such a sense of movement and space arises from his experience of throwing the discus.

Spear (javelin) throwing

With this gymnastic we change the plane of action. With the discus we unwound, spiralling out to the horizon and the discus, although given direction, is propelled out of a circling plane to an extension of a spreading action. The impression gained from the centrifugal pull of the discus releases us into a feeling of expanding in all directions to the horizon.

With the javelin the experience is totally different. It is a narrow action which consists of reaching back for the throw and coming forward. This narrow and directional action, together with the stepping back to draw power from that invisible area behind us, works into our movement memory as an inspiration for speaking. We imagine the impulse to speak as something that strikes us like a thought, which we receive and then deliver directly out into space. The memory of javelin throwing gives us an inner preparation for stage speaking, it becoming quite instinctive to feel the 'spear-throwing style' when delivering a speech.

The position of body, arm and hand when preparing to throw a javelin is seen to be correct or otherwise by the angle at which the javelin strikes the ground. You observe the position of the spear and then alter your hand position behind you for the next throw. Psychologically, this again directs the attention to the invisible area behind the actor, where the correct attitude, grasp and reception of the impulse to throw (or speak) dwells.

The extension of oneself back towards the area behind and then forward, provides the experience of a new plane of action.

Wrestling

Wrestling can help to enliven that activity which goes on 'below' the head—the 'wit' of the body, or rather, the wit of what moves the body. For in wrestling one learns to 'read' the activity of the other's will, as you feel him push or pull against your own grip and vice versa; also you react instinctively to what comes to meet you from your adversary. This brings power into the limbs, but the tension in the muscles is going outwards.

The tension which holds back, pulls in, however, is really of no value artistically, for it simply indicates some kind of fear in a person.

Tension which goes *outwards*, however, or pulls across, as one experiences it in wrestling, is an expanding, extending activity, which releases power in the actor's gesture, and also enables performers to contact each other across the area of the stage. Sometimes after wrestling we get a sense of free movement, like we get if we lean against a wall and press our arm firmly, and then step away—and our arm seems to fly up of its own volition.

With wrestling, the body begins to reveal a life of its own, an exuberant, expanding sensation, leading to that essential feeling for the actor on the stage, the feeling of buoyancy, as though one were supported by outer forces, as though the body and the gesture rested upon the space.

Such a sensation creates a feeling for the actor of filling the stage with activity. The actors when wrestling can at times separate but continue to feel the interplay of gesture across the acting area. In Chapter 8, we will study the subject of wrestling again, and see how we take it into the dynamic of speaking.

* * * * *

These are techniques that eventually can sink back into the instinctive life of the actor, and yet be ever present to provide him with the capacity to bring all his imagination into the space that lives outside himself, where he can truly work in closer participation with the spectator. So much of this work is aimed at providing the actor with the ability to discover his or her artistic instincts, to reawaken qualities which, either through education or convention, are ignored or are simply dormant.

EXERCISE: A MIME DEVELOPED FROM THE ACTIVITY OF WRESTLING

Two characters on either side of a river. The noise of the water drowns their voices, but the gesture of one seeks to encourage the other to cross the river on the stepping stones—the other indicates reluctance to do so. Their conversation is carried out in dumb show.

CHAPTER 4
Effective Speaking in the Theatre

In the last chapter we experienced the shifting of weight, balance, and adjustment of the body, as well as action without motive. And we have experienced the first stage of 'a sense of movement'. Now if the sensation of stepping, walking or running is transferred to speaking, we develop a lively form of articulation. We call it 'stepping through the line'. We can speak a line as though the words were like stepping-stones. This provides a basis for effective speaking in the theatre.

The following simple exercise illustrates how we develop the activity of stepping out, in speech, towards a partner. The actors stand in two rows facing each other; the wider the space between the two rows the better. The first line is spoken across the space to the performer opposite who then speaks to the next actor down the opposite row. He in turn speaks across to the next actor. So the sentence zig-zags down the rows. The next line is spoken by an actor at the head of the row and is again passed down.

> Are you speaking the truth?
> Of course I am.
> I am not so sure about that.
> You dare to say that to me.
> Who can stop me?
> I can.
> I've a good mind to go.
> Then go, and don't come back.
> Why should I want to?
> My pleasure.
> I will leave with him.
> Does anyone else wish to go?

Yes, I do.
And I.
Then leave.

As you deliver each line across the space, feel that you step out with each word. This will portray a sincerity and conviction as though these were your last words on the matter. You are now expressing a mood, not by finding it within yourself but by applying a technique. With this technique the words are not projected or pushed but live in the bubble of air that is the theatre. Later, in Chapter 9, we will look at the possibility of stepping consciously each syllable of a word.

It took me many years of performing in mimes and dance dramas to come to the final conclusion that it is the voice of the actor which grips the attention of the theatre audience. It is the power of the speaking which provides the platform for thought, the support to feeling and the general effectiveness of dramatic action.

Physical theatre, Grotowski, the Theatre of the Absurd, social realism and naturalism have all arisen in the dramatic field as the power and expression of speaking diminishes. Mime, with all its magical qualities, stands open-mouthed when we need to think or express more than the familiar, and only the addition of music can compensate in some measure for the loss of speech.

The theatre is neither for the dumb nor for the prosaic. Dialogue prevents us from being dumb and the quality of speaking prevents us from being prosaic.

Yet, there is little or no training in eloquence or rhetoric in the schools and colleges of our day, as there was in Elizabethan times. What a loss that is to education, to the social life and to the theatre. Let us imagine that most of the audience visiting a theatre nowadays had, in their basic education, received regular training in speaking. The actor would feel challenged, as he must have done in Shakespeare's time, when so many of the audience were trained speakers.

We are not talking of upper class speech or of the nicely turned phrase but of the quality of sound itself that the actor or actress produces in the theatre.

I am no great lover of opera, but when Pavarotti performed in

Hyde Park to an audience which covered the whole spectrum of social life in the country I felt that he had stolen a march on the actor. Why does drama not hold such power? What had so many come to see or hear? It was his voice. Though delivered in a manner completely in opposition to the techniques of speaking in the theatre, I could still appreciate the power of his voice. Not only was there the strength, but in his case the technique of passion. In the theatre we work with a different technique, but if developed it would also cause an audience to visit us from all walks of life to enjoy the human voice—a voice which did not sing, but spoke of ideas and thoughts, hopes and desires, the speech engendering an inner vitality in which the listener can bask. Living thoughts need living speech, and these two qualities combined create dramatic life and the world of drama.

What is the difference between everyday conversation and that performed on the stage? With the first, we think and express our thoughts. On the stage, we only call upon our memory. What we *present* is the process of thinking combined with speaking, but we do not actually do the thinking part. There is only the appearance of thought taking place as the words are spoken. In fact something quite different is happening. As the delivery of the line—'stepping through the line'—involves no thought, only the pretence of thought, so the speaking is free to respond entirely to the will of the actor. Therefore it becomes effective, 'will-full' speech. This kind of speaking stimulates the interest of our fellow humans, who become alert when they hear effective speaking. The very style itself arouses interest and attention.

The actor of today apparently has only one task; to play the character convincingly. Nevertheless, he should be aware of another task, and that is to preserve a quality of speaking which responds sympathetically to the listener. Speaking in the theatre should not include qualities so often heard in life—the tense, constricted speech of anxiety, a hard tone, aggressive speaking, and so forth. Although we may portray these qualities on the stage, we have to ensure that our speech only gives the *impression* of harsh sounds, which should never be inflicted on the audience in actuality. In conveying a character's speaking, you should only act the manner of it, though the laws of speech must still be maintained, with the sound flowing out on the breath in a free, unconstricted way.

Imagine that the theatre architecture supports our speech, for it lives in the centre of the building where the audience sit. Gordon Craig's architectural scenery possesses this supportive quality. The actor has this double task, first of portraying a character who may indeed, out of the situation, use his speech in a wild and hysterical way, and secondly, while this portrayal must be convincing, the techniques of speaking have to remain immune to the demands of the drama. In other words, we act the drama but leave a space within our work to allow the speaking to survive. This is where we come back to our spear throwing (see pp. 28-9); the educationalist Rudolf Steiner described how the ancient Greeks included spear throwing in their gymnastics to develop good public speaking.

Preparation, Action and Completion in speech and gesture

However mundane an action upon the stage, it must contain the Preparation, the Action and the Completion.

Preparation

Often the phrase 'thought before action' is used in order to disguise the mere speaking of the printed word. To grasp the idea of preparation we must return once more to our description of spear throwing. When we reach back, the spear is behind us in the throwing posture. It is *how* we hold the spear at that moment, that determines the flight, the accuracy of impact and the angle of the spear when it strikes the ground. Therefore, 'preparation' could in this instance be considered almost as the total activity of judgement and decision, whereas what follows is merely the activity of the human will executing the decisions arrived at in the thinking and feeling of the spear thrower, or actor.

After the moment of preparation, the spear—or the gesture, or the word—is released. The thinking that took place in the moment of moving forward towards releasing the spear now becomes quiescent. All is now in the will of the performer, with perhaps slight adjustment from the feeling.

One could almost say that a major purpose of rehearsal is to discover what you wish to *prepare* to deliver. For the spear thrower, it is a comparatively slow process of preparation, but for the speaker or actor it is often a very quick process, which—when resolved into action—immediately calls for the next preparation, of the next phrase or gesture.

Therefore, in our 'speech-dances' (which we will go into fully in Chapter 6), the dancer must always prepare the gesture a moment before his speaking partner delivers the line, and in so doing he discovers a way of memorizing his preparations.

Action

When the actor knows exactly what he intends to do throughout a speech and consciously carries out his intentions, a most stimulating impression of spontaneity appears, even if he is a little pedantic at first, even if, during practice, he has to think for a moment of the transition to his next attitude, gesture or inflexion. When he delivers the line as a free deed of feeling and will, the action then appears to have arisen from himself in that very moment. The more conscious you are of what you are doing, the more spontaneous the effect.

Completion

We have spoken about Rudolf Laban's abhorrence of the shadow gesture. This objection is most valid in a theatrical performance, for what we do upon the stage is reflected in the inner life of the spectator. In my experience an incomplete action can be curiously damaging to a performance and, one suspects, to the audience as well. It is as though we prepare to throw a javelin, we then throw it and quite suddenly we lose interest before it has completed its flight. We could say such shadow gestures indicate a weakness in the decisive quality of the actor and can also disturb the will-life of the spectator. To counteract this tendency, an actor may, for example, reach for a pen—an action complete in itself; he will pick up the pen—again a complete action; he will sign a document—a complete action; and then return the pen back to the tray—a final complete action.

The character portrayed in the play may not be particularly decisive. Therefore, the actor must disguise the four episodes, make them seem casual, mundane. Nevertheless, the discipline is *within* the action.

When he has completed an action, for a brief moment he has created a space before the next action begins. This space is a vital part of the action, as important as the action itself, because it allows a new impulse or decision to enter into the performance. Thus, two violinists may perform rapid arpeggios in turn; one violinist travels from one note to another without sensing the infinitesimal space *between* each note. Such a fault can be very noticeable. The second, on the other hand, may play with a sense that each note is a *new impulse*—and this too will come across.

To complete a deed is to allow for a new preparation; if we fail to sense the freedom that comes from having completed an action, we run the risk of a certain element of staleness spoiling the work. In terms of the metaphor of spear throwing, it is as if one is just *stabbing* with the spear, instead of releasing the spear and reaching back to collect another spear. The reaching back is a passive gesture—it is the new spear which is important. This applies, of course, equally to gesture and to speech.

Letting light shine through speech

What has been described above is no complicated gymnastic, although it may appear so when merely described in words. If, in fact, this sequence—completion, release, reaching back, collecting, preparation, delivery—can be imagined as so natural as to become a way of life for the actor, then the drama may perhaps recapture the same creative energy which lives on in the sister art of music.

Imagine a violin being played so that the notes slur across each other. It can be the same way in speech, although we are so

36

habituated to slurred speech that it now seems natural to us.

From seeking spaces between the phrases, we can go on to find space between the words, and thence, as we really become dexterous with our tongue and perceptive with our ears, we begin to discover space between syllables. In so doing, we are making speech *transparent*—that is to say, we are letting light shine through the speech. This requires the same sort of agility and concentration as that practised by musicians.

Not only in speech, but also in thought and movement, such instances of release and preparation are like chinks of light penetrating the dark coils of unrelieved action and speech.

EXERCISE: THE STYLE OF THE SPEAR THROWER

This style is an essential for speaking. Let us start from the sentence, or phrase. We have a thought, either our own or one written down in a playscript. We think, we speak. We have another thought or, in the script, another phrase, but between each thought or phrase it is necessary to have a space, that is, a receptive moment, before the next thought appears in speech.

This process is linked with the preparation that we spoke of in this chapter. If one releases one idea and imagines that one calls in another, something of the truth of thinking and feeling shows in the performance. During practice you can speak the first complete thought, then turn completely around. As you face your partner again, speak the next thought. The turning-around is a way of releasing one thought and collecting the next. This process of release and new impulse clarifies thought and delivery.

We can perhaps imagine each new idea shooting downwards from above like a dart, stimulating us into action. The build-up of thoughts is very apparent in Hamlet's 'To be or not to be'. Try this speech as though Hamlet is, as we say, 'struck' by a thought, and then another. This is an excellent exercise for releasing the passing thought and catching another. ▶

FROM *HAMLET* ACT III, SCENE I

HAMLET. To be, or not to be, that is the question:
Whether 'tis nobler in the mind to suffer
The slings and arrows of outrageous Fortune,
Or to take arms against a sea of troubles,
And by opposing end them: to die to sleep;
No more; and by sleep, to say we end
The heart-ache and the thousand natural shocks
That flesh is heir to? 'tis a consummation
Devoutly to be wish'd. To die, to sleep,
To sleep, perchance to dream; ay, there's the rub,
For in that sleep of death, what dreams may come,
When we have shuffled off this mortal coil,
Must give us pause.

Breathing: an ingredient of speech

Today we store breath; it is even a technique for speaking. We store breath and then release it, as though rationing it for future use. This style of breathing lives with us in our daily experience; we can breathe in, but find it more difficult to breathe out; we are inhalers.

This holding onto the breath is also psychological. We so often save something, hold back, withdraw. Our very speech is restrained and presses against a deep instinct not to release. The actor expresses emotion by apparently restraining it. We guess what the emotion may be by his disguise of it, and if he then has to release pent-up feelings, according to the demands of the play, a deep resistance to such a demand causes him to wrestle with his voice and force it out against, it would seem, his inclination. This is not a criticism of actors for it is deeply embedded in our modern cultural life. To release the word on the breath almost calls for a complete reappraisal of one's entire life-style. When our feelings, thoughts and actions are released and become words, the communication so desperately sought for today will become a reality.

Conversation

What is needed in stage conversation? Imagine, as in the exercise on p. 30, that you are beside a river across which are stepping stones and a timid character stands on the other side. Because of the noise of the rushing river you are only able to communicate by gesture with the other person, whom you try to persuade to cross. This develops for us an eye-to-eye link across the stage and a feeling that our gesture extends beyond our fingertips not only to our fellow performers on-stage but to the audience as well.

We will bring our gesture into speaking with a small duologue. Again the partners are as far apart as is possible.

A You over there! Yes, you! Go and fetch the broom!

B Are you speaking to me? Go and fetch it yourself.

A Steady now. Just get the broom for me.

B Get it yourself. I'm busy.

A If you do not obey me I have no alternative but to ask you to leave.

B Try it. I'm too useful around here.

A It wouldn't appear so.

B Ask others.

A I have.

—and so on. One can improvise such scenes, but always carry out the preparation of a spear thrower before you speak; not only is it the taking in of breath but also the feeling of collecting the next thought to deliver on the stream of breath. Suppose we look at the speech on p. 40 from Shakespeare's *Henry V*. You have decided how you will interpret the speech and character, so all you have now is to concern yourself with the technique of speaking. The way the lines are set out—in iambic pentameters—indicates the pattern of delivery, but when you have reached the end of one line you will have the feeling that you have to perform some nimble gymnastic in order to be ready for the next.

39

'In peace there's nothing so becomes a man'

Now perform in your mind a swift movement which takes you from the last word of the line into the first word of the following line.

'As modest stillness and humility'

In Shakespeare's writing, King Henry does not let his or the listening soldiers' attention relax, so neither must you when speaking the part. Henry must hurl his enthusiasm beyond the end of each line in order to catch them for the next line. It is like relay racing; the end of the line is only passing on the baton, it is not the end of the race. You neither run the lines together in a naturalistic way nor stop at the end of a line in a mechanical way, but inwardly perform with speed and alacrity invisible gestures to bring you into the next line. Thus the listening audience will feel the unity of the verse in thought and action beyond mere naturalistic delivery.

To put it another way, Henry must maintain in the silences an inner activity in order to maintain the concentration of the listening soldiers. The silences should be an effective part of the speech rather than 'dead' moments.

KING HENRY V, Act III, Scene I

KING HENRY. Once more unto the breach, dear friends, once
        more;
    Or close the wall up with our English dead!
    In peace there's nothing so becomes a man
    As modest stillness and humility:
    But when the blast of war blows in our ears,
    Then imitate the action of the tiger;
    Stiffen the sinews, summon up the blood,
    Disguise fair nature with hard-favour'd rage;
    Then lend the eye a terrible aspect;
    Let it pry through the portage of the head
    Like the brass cannon; let the brow o'erwhelm it
    As fearfully as doth a galled rock

40

O'erhang and jutty his confounded base,
Swill'd with the wild and wasteful ocean.
Now set the teeth and stretch the nostril wide,
Hold hard the breath, and bend up very spirit
To his full height! On, on, you noblest English!
Whose blood is fet from fathers of war-proof;
Fathers that, like so many Alexanders,
Have in these parts from morn to even fought,
And sheath'd their swords for lack of argument.
Dishonour not your mothers; now attest
That those whom you call'd fathers did beget you.
Be copy now to men of grosser blood,
And teach them how to war. And you, good yeomen,
Whose limbs were made in England, show us here
The mettle of your pasture; let us swear
That you are worth your breeding; which I doubt not;
For there is none of you so mean and base
That hath not noble lustre in your eyes.
I see you stand like greyhounds in the slips,
Straining upon the start. The game's afoot:
Follow your spirit; and upon this charge
Cry 'God for Harry! England and Saint George!'

We will now unite all that we have spoken of into a small scene,
between four characters. The actors and actresses sit or stand as
far apart as possible on the stage. Each character will prepare and
deliver the lines towards one of the other three characters. Try to
feel that they reach the other character by stepping through space
not only with the content of the line but with the spoken words.
We have both stepping through the line and the preparation and
delivery of the spear thrower. Finally, the invisible gymnastics of
preparation bring the next line into the right place for the
delivery. We must of course take into account the simple
statements the characters make but also feel behind the naturalism of the scene a great deal of invisible activity. I had the
opportunity to work with Rudolf Laban, whose 'Art of Movement' techniques and theories became so much a part of the world
of dance. He would speak of the contact he believed he could see
between people as they spoke in conversation. When a group

spoke together, he believed he could see a net of activity being woven between the group as they exchanged ideas. So I have called this simple scene 'The Net'.

THE NET

A   Why don't you stay at home more, you're always out.

B   Why shouldn't I be?

C   Your mother's right.

D   Quiet Dad, just leave it alone!

C   Don't you treat me like some second-class citizen.

B   What's the point of staying at home when we have to listen to all this rubbish.

A   Doreen, be quiet!

B   Well, I mean it. You only want me here in order to take your side when you have a fight with father.

C   Don't interfere with our life, young lady.

D   Why, because you don't interfere with ours?

C   Well, do we? Do we interfere with your life? No, we don't. All your mother was asking was that you should both stay in some time. Keep the family together.

D   Keep the family together! You've always made such a thing about how the children broke up the family. How the family sacrificed so much, to bring the children up.

C   Well, it's true.

A   Now you can repay us by staying at home a little, to keep us company.

D   What is all this about the family, keeping you company and so on?

B	Yes, what is all this? What are you both so nervous about?
D	Don't you two like to be left alone any more?
C	What are you implying by that remark?
B	He's not implying, he's asking a good question.
C	Your mum and I have nothing to be nervous about.
D	Maybe it's the thought of sitting here gazing at each other hour after hour.
A	That's a cruel and unnecessary remark.
B	Isn't it touching, Robert, to see Mum and Dad clinging to one another.
A	Doreen, you know that your father has his little ways, same as we all have, and that we all have to learn to live with each other. That is why we want you to stay at home a little more. We don't know you.
B	That's true.
D	And you don't want to know us.
C	That's true. There's nothing to know. You've become a waste of time, both to us and yourselves.
A	Father, don't say that.
C	Whose side are you on? You know that is what we both think.
A	No, we don't, we don't.
D	Make up your minds.
B	It's worth staying at home just to hear what you both think of us.
C	Be quiet. Edith, you know we are worried about them both.

D	Oh, so now it is worried is it? You're worried about us.
A	Yes, that's true. We have been worried. You see we feel you have no base, no home, no settled place where you can, er . . . rest.
C	Where you can think and plan your lives.
A	Instead of rushing about filling up your time with nothingness.
D	And what do you fill your time up with?
C	Worrying about you.
B	We're all right. We have our own lives, our own friends. Whatever we have—which isn't much, I'd admit, but it's what we have to build on—it's our own.
D	You know Dad, we sometimes worry about you. We really do.
B	So there are the four of us, worrying about each other.
A	In a way it is a comfort. Between members of a family there is no distance or time. Wherever we are, we can somehow share thoughts.
C	The fact is, they are never here. We've lost them. That is the truth.
D	We also have lost you, Mum. We lost you both years ago, long before you thought you had lost us.
B	Now can we go out tonight?
A	Yes, of course.
B	Dad?
C	Yes, but don't think that we never think of you. You're never out of our minds.

D	We even need to be free of that, Dad. Free of your minds.
A	If it's possible, we'll try that also. Only because we love you.
B	Hate holds people together. Love lets them be free.
C	All right, all right, out you go.
D and B	Goodnight.
A and C	Goodnight.

Speaking Like Ghosts

We shall return to the subject of speech later in the book. I now conclude this chapter with the scene between Hamlet and the spirit of his father. The Ghost can only influence Hamlet by his speaking. He cannot grab him by the collar and put physical pressure upon him, but by his delivery he can surround and hold Hamlet and force him to listen. So if the actor playing the Ghost believes that his only control over Hamlet is through his breath and the forming of his speech he will appreciate how the power of delivery has a place within the theatre. Behind all our work we speak like ghosts to the audience and our only real hold over their attention is through the dynamic, gymnastic activity of the speech in the auditorium.

HAMLET, ACT I, SCENE V

HAMLET. Where wilt thou lead me? speak; I'll go no further.

GHOST. Mark me.

HAMLET. I will.

GHOST. My hour is almost come,
    When I to sulphurous and tormenting flames
    Must render up myself.

HAMLET. Alas poor ghost.

45

GHOST. Pity me not, but lend thy serious hearing
  To what I shall unfold.

HAMLET. Speak, I am bound to hear.

GHOST. So art thou to revenge, when thou shalt hear.

HAMLET. What?

GHOST. I am thy father's spirit,
  Doom'd for a certain term to walk the night,
  And for the day confin'd to fast in fires,
  Till the foul crimes done in my days of nature
  Are burnt and purged away. But that I am forbid
  To tell the secrets of my prison-house,
  I could a tale unfold whose lightest word
  Would harrow up thy soul, freeze they young blood
  Make thy two eyes, like stars, start from their spheres,
  Thy knotty and combined locks to part,
  And each particular hair to stand on end,
  Like quills upon the fretful porpentine:
  But this eternal blazon must not be
  To ears of flesh and blood. List, list, O list!
  If thou didst ever thy dear father love—

HAMLET. O God!

GHOST. Revenge his foul and most unnatural murder.

HAMLET. Murder!

GHOST. Murder most foul, as in the best it is;
  But this most foul, strange and unnatural.

HAMLET. Haste, me to know't, that I with wings as swift
  As meditation, or the thoughts of love,
  May sweep to my revenge.

GHOST. I find thee apt;
  And duller shouldst thou be than the fat weed
  That roots itself in ease on Lethe wharf,
  Wouldn't thou not stir in this. Now Hamlet hear:
  'Tis given out that, sleeping in my orchard,
  A serpent stung me: so the whole ear of Denmark,

Is by a forged process of my death
Rankly abus'd: but know thou noble youth,
The serpent that did sting thy father's life,
Now wears his crown.

HAMLET. O my prophetic soul!
My uncle!

GHOST. Ay that incestuous, that adulterate beast,
With witchcraft of his wit, with traitorous gifts—
O wicked wit, and gifts, that have the power
So to seduce!—won to his shameful lust
The will of my most seeming-virtuous queen:
O Hamlet, what a falling-off was there!
From me, whose love was of that dignity,
That it went hand in hand, even with the vow
I made to her in marriage; and to decline
Upon a wretch whose natural gifts were poor
To those of mine!
But virtue, as it never will be moved,
Though lewdness court it in a shape of heaven,
So lust, though to a radiant angel link'd,
Will sate itself in a celestial bed,
And prey on garbage.
But soft! methinks I scent the morning's air;
Brief let me be: sleeping within my orchard,
My custom always in the afternoon,
Upon my secure hour thy uncle stole
With juice of cursed hebenon in a vial,
And in the porches of mine ears did pour
The leperous distilment; whose effect
Holds such an enmity with blood of man
That swift as quicksilver it courses through
The natural gates and alleys of the body;
And with a sudden vigour it doth posset
And curd, like eager droppings into milk,
The thin and wholesome blood: so did it mine
And a most instant tetter bark'd about,
Most lazar-like, with vile and loathsome crust,
All my smooth body.

47

Thus was I, sleeping, by a brother's hand,
Of life, of crown, and queen, at once dispatch'd;
Cut off even in the blossoms of my sin,
Unhousel'd, disappointed, unaneled.
No reckoning made, but sent to my account
With all my imperfections on my head;
O horrible! O horrible! most horrible!
If thou hast nature in thee bear it not;
Let not the royal bed of Denmark be
A couch for luxury and damned incest.
But howsoever thou pursuest this act,
Taint not thy mind, nor let thy soul contrive
Against thy mother aught; leave her to heaven,
And to those thorns that in her bosom lodge,
To prick and sting her. Fare thee well at once!
The glow-worm shows the matin to be near,
And 'gins to pale his uneffectual fire;
Adieu, adieu! Hamlet, remember me.

Exit.

CHAPTER 5
The Wind Machine

Imagine that a high wind is blowing through the room—that the room is a kind of wind-tunnel. Into this tunnel we step and are immediately picked up and spun down the length of the room. Although this is acting, the feeling of being lifted and carried across the room is nevertheless a very real one. We should now guide this sense of buoyancy through a series of gestures such as those set out in the list below. Always feel you are carried on a stream of air. This sensation we call the 'overwhelming' gesture.

Overwhelming
Looking
Listening
Fearful
Joyful
Finding
In Aladdin's cave
Enthusiasm
Amazed
Successful

As we grow familiar with this experience we can slightly resist the force that is carrying us and so form stronger gestures. We begin to resist and push against the wind. So first we are carried into the centre of the hall or stage, and then we turn and push against the wind. Perhaps we fall back and begin to be carried away again but resist and push. From this simple exercise we begin to get a feeling of being 'overwhelmed' or of 'asserting'. We can transform the pressing or pushing against the wind into gestures that are of a different mood.

Asserting
Triumphant
Commanding
Searching
Challenging
Overseeing
A Revolutionary
Defiant
Successful

First, we perform them out of our imagination and very much out of ourselves. Then the exercises should be repeated, but *copying* what was done before. You mentally stand outside yourself and begin to carry out the gestures as though it was someone else performing. We begin to experience acting—for the action becomes conscious, and this adds a strength and a sense of performance to the work. I have always found that the second 'copying' demonstration has a fresh and inventive quality to it which was not there in the first mime. That, however, is for the spectators to decide.

Finally, a group of actors and actresses can represent a family struggling against a high wind or sandstorm. Some characters push themselves against the wind and drag others with them. Some others are carried away, too weak to push, and they drag others back with them, and so forth. This sequence develops into a drama that underlies many stage plays.

This next scene has no literary or even dramatic merit, but it was written out of the two elements we have been discussing, asserting/overwhelming. Try and work out of these two elements in the scene bringing the sense of outer activity—the wind blowing—into the speaking. One character is obviously overwhelmed and the other assertive.

EXERCISE: WIND-BLOWING SCENE

A [*speaking on the telephone*] No! No! You must not phone me at this number. I've told you. I made it quite clear, you must not ring me here. If you . . .

[*Hastily sets down phone looking guilty and apprehensive*]

50

[Enter B]

B What's going on?

A Oh, they have just rung to say that the whole arrangement is off, that someone has written and cancelled our contract with them. It's most mysterious.

B There is no mystery. I cancelled the contract.

A You did?

B Yes.

A But why?

B Because I don't trust you.

A I don't understand.

B I suspect that you are not being entirely honest with me. I think that you are planning to involve me in a complicated financial arrangement, and that when I have to borrow money in order to fulfil the contract you will tell them I'm a financial risk and they will then blackmail and threaten me into a new agreement.

A Why should you think I would do such a thing? I don't understand you. Have you gone mad? Why have you invented such a wicked story? There is no reason for me to cheat, no point or purpose. I gain nothing by destroying our own business. Why are you behaving like this?

B Give me the contract.

A I haven't got it.

B Where is it?

A Why do you want it?

B To see if you've changed it, behind my back.

A Why should I?

B Don't argue. Give me the contract.

51

A I don't know where it is.

B The contract!

A You must be either joking with me or quite mad.

B The contract!

A I tell you, it must be in the bank. It's not here. I left it with the bank. Why are you treating me like this?

B Give me the contract. If you don't, then I must believe that you've rewritten it to your advantage.

A I haven't got it. I haven't seen it since we last discussed it. You said we should put it in the bank. It was your idea. Yes, I remember now, you said quite clearly, 'put it in the bank', so I did. Now, when was it? Last Thursday—no, Tuesday. Yes, I remember . . .

B Go to hell.   [*Exit B*]

A [*breathless, goes to the telephone and dials*] He suspects. He knows, everything, everything!

[*Rings off*]

The next scene is from Shakespeare's *Othello*. I believe it contains something of that 'wind-blowing' quality. I hope you can find it. Play the characters in whatever way you will, but let us agree, for the exercise, that Desdemona is overwhelmed by Othello's behaviour and Othello is 'assertive' in his judgement of her. Allow the invisible gesture to appear in voice and gesture.

FROM *OTHELLO*, ACT III, SCENE IV

OTHELLO. How do you, Desdemona?

DESDEMONA. Well, my good lord.

OTHELLO. Give me you hand: this hand is moist, my lady.

DESDEMONA. It yet hath felt no age nor known no sorrow.

OTHELLO. This argues fruitfulness and liberal heart;
   Hot, hot, and moist: this hand of yours requires
   A sequester from liberty, fasting and prayer,
   Much castigation, exercise devout;
   For here's a young and sweating devil here,
   That commonly rebels. 'Tis a good hand,
   A frank one.

DESDEMONA. You may, indeed, say so;
   For 'twas that hand that gave away my heart.

OTHELLO. A liberal hand: the hearts of old gave hands;
   But our new heraldry is hands, not hearts.

DESDEMONA. I cannot speak of this. Come now, your promise.

OTHELLO. What promiso, chuck?

DESDEMONA. I have sent to bid Cassio come speak with you.

OTHELLO. I have a salt and sorry rheum offends me;
   Lend me thy handkerchief.

DESDEMONA. Here, my lord.

OTHELLO. That which I gave you.

DESDEMONA. I have it not about me.

OTHELLO. Not?

DESDEMONA. No, indeed, my lord.

OTHELLO. That is a fault.
   That handkerchief
   Did an Egyptian to my mother give;
   She was a charmer, and could almost read
   The thoughts of people: she told her, while she kept it,
   'Twould make her amiable, and subdue my father
   Entirely to her love; but if she lost it,
   Or made a gift of it, my father's eye
   Should hold her loathed, and his spirits should hunt
   After new fancies: she, dying, gave it me;
   And bid me, when my fate would have me wive,

To give it her. I did so: and take heed on't,
Make it a darling like your precious eye;
To lose't or give't away were such perdition
As nothing else could match.

DESDEMONA. Is't possible?

OTHELLO. 'Tis true; there's magic in the web of it;
A sibyl, that had number'd in the world
The sun to course two hundred compasses,
In her prophetic fury sew'd the work;
The worms were hallow'd that did breed the silk;
And it was dyed in mummy which the skilful
Conserv'd of maidens' hearts.

DESDEMONA. Indeed! is't true?

OTHELLO. Most veritable; therefore look to 't well.

DESDEMONA. Then would to God that I had never seen't!

OTHELLO. Ha! wherefore?

DESDEMONA. Why do you speak so startingly and rash?

OTHELLO. Is't lost? is't gone? speak; is it out o' the way?

DESDEMONA. Heaven bless us!

OTHELLO. Say you?

DESDEMONA. It is not lost; but what an if it were?

OTHELLO. How!

DESDEMONA. I say, it is not lost.

OTHELLO. Fetch't let me see 'it.

DESDEMONA: Why, so I can, sir, but I will not now.
This is a trick to put me from my suit:
Pray you, let Cassio be receiv'd again.

OTHELLO. Fetch me the handkerchief: my mind misgives.

DESDEMONA. Come, come;
You'll never meet a more sufficient man.

OTHELLO. The handkerchief!

DESDEMONA. I pray, talk me of Cassio.

OTHELLO. The handkerchief!

DESDEMONA. A man that all his time
Hath founded his good fortune on your love,
Shared dangers with you—

OTHELLO. The handkerchief!

DESDEMONA. In sooth, you are to blame.

OTHELLO. Away!

Exit

The Approach of an Emotion

A friend of mine is a keen mountaineer. He once described to me an experience he had when climbing. It was during a particularly hazardous part of the climb and he became aware, as he shifted himself slowly along the cliff face, that from far way fear was approaching. He sensed it, far out in space. Then fear was beginning to move—to move nearer and nearer. While part of him concentrated on the climbing another part of him was fully occupied holding back fear, knowing that upon its arrival he would 'freeze' to the cliff and become a hazard to his friends. He devoted almost all his energy to holding fear at bay, until he reached a resting place. Now this experience of a feeling or emotion approaching a person, which will either take over or be repelled by him, has something to say to the actor.

Let us experiment with the idea that feelings approach the human being leaving him a choice in how to deal with them. I have set down some rather dramatic speeches for the actor/listener to dance to and gesture, as a colleague reads them. The latter can whisper these thoughts into the actor's ear, who will then react as though speaking to himself. Remember, while doing these, the 'Underwater' exercise on p. 10.

UNDERWATER SEQUENCE

CHORUS. [Anxiety: grey water, cold but swift]

Oh, anxiety torments me: my regrets for the past, my fear of today, and the terror, the dreadful terror of tomorrow. What comes to meet me I fear most of all. I cannot see it, yet, I feel its pressure. I know it is approaching, I feel its weight and, if I listen, it hoarsely whispers in my ear dreadful tidings the burden of which will, I know, crush and destroy me. Oh, the humiliation of failure, to live with the unlivable—for now I know that disaster rushes towards me. The voice warns me, haunts me, squeezes my soul into a knot of fear.

[Hope: sun on the surface of sea]

And yet, something tells me that this night of my soul is lying to me—it is not true! There is no darkness, only that of my own fashioning. How can one not believe that the future can only be glorious? Whatever the adventures of life bring us, the future must be glorious just by being the future. Then let us face the sun and welcome what is to come.

[Anger: heavy swell]

Why should I have to encourage myself, fighting illusion with illusion, resisting the fearsome with poetic fancy? Is this God's message to Man, that we should battle and strenuously savage our doubts and fears? Is our anger our only possession? Is torment the order of the day, and escape through illusions our true fate—to rage and curse at what we cannot see and yet experience? To recognize as a dream—from which we will awake again and again—to shout at our own fears. Are we nothing but a parcel of groans, self-engendered, spending our lives like a dog, snapping at our own tail?

[Humour: sparkling sea]

What a little speech, full of rich and purple prose—what you need is a tiny feather to tickle up your nose. What a bore; what a jaw. It is essential, quintessential and double quintessential to muckle spread your life with mocking laughter. This was God's plan, to create a funny man. A fickle, funny, simple, sunny, pickled, stippled, funny man. That's God's plan.

[Loneliness: grey, still water. Cold]
The Cathedral of Loneliness, echoing the pale cry of a ghostly waif, fragile soul, wispy human. How pitiful it is not to be loved. A little unlovable. God's yawn. Is it my fault that I have no friend, no companion? No! There are those in life who are born to despair. The stupid world rushes by leaving the delicate, purer part of itself to wander, unrecognized and unloved, upon the plains of time. We lonely ones are the victims of others' stupidity. We are the martyrs of society. We carry the stern burden of responsibility. We are the hidden depths; we are nature's compensation for the shallow waters of the world.

[Mocking: turbulent sea]
The rash courage of ribald rebellion splashes life into the dull torments of philosophers. Splash and stir the surface and aggravate the depths. Spill the substance of our energy upon the static, blank face of nature. For we know what we are—we are free men. No one can tell us anything, for we learn from experience—our inner experience. From this we judge. So we must experience the world, experience everything, everywhere. Turmoil is life; stillness is death. We live and live, swirling and swallowing, whirling and wallowing. For we exist and that is enough.

[Peaceful: placid sea]
Serene face, that contemplates all that has past and smiles upon the challenge of the future. How sweet is peace that even in the face of robust rebellion can smile on the tiger, and appreciate its power and energy, knowing that one day, through experience, it too will find that powerful peace it so admires. Tranquillity is passive but peace is positive. It glides with purpose awake and alert, not lost in a hasty dream.

The following is the same exercise but with superior writing.

FROM *HAMLET*, ACT II, SCENE II

HAMLET. O, what a rogue and peasant slave am I!
Is it not monstrous that this player here,

But in a fiction, in a dream of passion,
Could force his soul so to his own conceit
That from her working all his visage wann'd,
Tears in his eyes, distraction in's aspect,
A broken voice, and his whole function suiting
With forms to his conceit? And all for nothing!
For Hecuba!
What's Hecuba to him, or he to Hecuba,
That he should weep for her? What would he do,
Had he the motive and the cue for passion
That I have? He would drown the stage with tears
And cleave the general ear with horrid speech,
Make mad the guilty and appal the free,
Confound the ignorant and amaze indeed
The very faculties of eyes and ears.
Yet I,
A dull and muddy-mettled rascal, peak,
Like John-a-dreams, unpregnant of my cause,
And can say nothing; no, not for a king,
Upon whose property and most dear life
A damned defeat was made . . .

These approaching emotions we have been discussing are often
described in our language—A thought struck me—Suspicion was
aroused—Pity overwhelmed me—I was burdened by depres-
sion—Gripped by hate—Anger choked me—Haunted with
dread—Curiosity impelled me—Overcome by despair. We can
invite jealousy, cast out envy, be heavy hearted, light hearted,
stung with remorse, tormented by doubts, cold with fear, hot
with shame, and so on. These forces seem to exert their influence
upon us from infinite space. Gordon Craig's settings for drama
invites this feeling of infinity where the action lives between the
'particular and the universal'.

Part of a speech from the play *The Dresser* by Ronald Harwood,
1980 (Amber Lane Press):

'SIR. *[the actor speaks of his performances of King Lear]* . . . I
thought tonight I caught sight of him. Or saw myself as he sees

me. Speaking 'Reason not the need', I was suddenly detached from myself. My thoughts flew. And I was observing from a great height. Go on, you bastard, I seemed to be saying or hearing. Go on, you've more to give, don't hold back, more, more, more. And I was watching Lear. Each word he spoke was fresh invented. I had no knowledge of what came next, what fate awaited him. The agony was in the moment of acting created. I saw an old man and the old man was me. And I knew there was more to come. But what? Bliss, partial recovery, more pain and death. All this I knew I had yet to see. Outside myself, do you understand? Outside myself . . .'

EXERCISE: THE MARIONETTE

Peripheral action

Imagine that like a marionette one is on strings, pulled this way and that. Then imagine one frees oneself from the strings, yet the pulling sensation remains. One is now pulled or pushed as by an outside agency. The nimble mover feels supported by the space and moves from outside himself. I have always thought Chaplin's brilliance lay in this innate sense that the space around him was living and vibrant.

Again like a marionette, the actor is pulled up. Gradually he frees himself from the strings, enjoys a time of freedom and then is again held by the strings. This heightens awareness of the surrounding space, including that vital area behind him that is so often ignored, that 'back awareness'.

Feel that the impulse to move comes from outside, not from your centre; feel that you are supported by the world around you.

EXERCISE: ATTRACTION, REPULSION

This is another exercise in space awareness—to realize the power of attraction and repulsion.

Imagine that in the early years of this century, for the first time, a tractor has been delivered to a farm. As the workers approach it, it attracts and then repulses; it appears beautiful or perhaps dangerous. It is a strange monster. Again they are attracted, and again they are fearful and step back, and so on.

The activity for the actor is that first he goes out to the object and then it works back upon him. It can happen that a building or a personal object can at one time be attractive, but then, because of some event, it suddenly proves repellent.

The object or the tractor must work upon the actor in this exercise and the student must truly feel the object attracting him or pushing him away. This expands the performer's ability to relate to the outside world and work from it, instead of purely from his own centre.

The Continuous Gesture

To create a mood, say of *suspicion*, let the actor express it, and then begin to travel around the stage area while maintaining the gesture. It is almost like a slow dance.

From this exercise of sustained gesture one begins to feel that to maintain the gesture the actor must be inwardly pouring in the mental energy that created the gesture. An intense sense of concentration is needed to sustain the gesture and mood. Then follows a reciprocal action. The physical gesture one is carrying out begins to reflect back into the performer's imagination, and the gesture begins to support itself. This moment when the gesture begins to have a life of its own is a most important one. For he approaches that boundary between subjective and objective action. When the gesture, because of his effort to maintain it, begins to assume a life of its own, it is as though a guided flow of energy directs the gesture. It begins to live outside of the actor and so become an objective medium for him to use as he wishes.

From this experience we begin to develop the consciousness of our own actions. For example: an actor may lean forward across a table, resting his weight on his hands, in order to emphasize something he is saying. As he does this, the very gesture tells him something about itself. As we carry these actions out we become conscious of our own deeds. Artistically this provides him with the means whereby he makes judgements.

Objectifying the Performance

We have progressed from the imagination of the story-teller, through his emphatic speaking, into the gesture of the actor. From the actor's innate sense of movement, we have sought back for the flowing gesture in the spoken thought. I have hinted at the possibility of conveying enhanced meaning through the dynamics of speaking, and grasping the meaning through active listening, by dancing the sentence.

As an exercise, perform a series of mimes involving strength, energy and tension—carrying heavy weights, getting angry, becoming fearful—with ease and suppleness of muscle, so that the strength and tension only are apparent. This can awaken an objective consciousness of actions being carried out.

To give an example of this consciousness let us hark back to the mountain-climbing incident mentioned on p. 55. If you are climbing a cliff, and become anxious and afraid because you have ventured too far, you may have a few brief moments of consciousness of the whole situation, such as the feeling 'I'm going to fall', or 'I'm beginning to feel ill with fear', but for the most part you are totally engrossed in the situation. To objectify it would somehow place you in greater mental danger.

One could say that in the extremity of fear you became fear itself, but did not experience it objectively. But in order to act out such a situation, the tension and anxiety is in fact objectified. One can experience the action *more* consciously than when suffering it in 'real life'.

Another exercise is for an actor to portray a soldier fighting for his life, with as much vigour and physical effort as the actor can muster. The soldier dies, but his ghost rises and continues to fight, but without the deep involvement of the physical effort. The actor picturing himself as the ghost performs the same deeds but with a certain transparency in the effort.

This creates in him the right feeling for acting. By objectifying the movement gently, he can perform the action and still remain completely conscious of it.

If I compose music there comes a time when it must stand by itself. A symphony may bear the name of the composer, and we may respect the composer for what he has created, but it stands by itself as a creation. The composer might even be glad to be rid of it, to let it go. He may say something like 'I have done with it', just as Matisse said 'Now my bags are packed,' on completing the interior of the chapel at Vence, shortly before his death.

This splendid objective possibility of art is not so easy to attain for the actor. He is too closely linked with his work. For his art, what he has to use is *himself*. Yet it is not inconceivable that his art may also become something that stands on its own, if only the right technique can be found.

An experienced actor, having played a given role fifty or a hundred times would come to sense that the play, and his own performance within the play, was—from repetition alone—assuming a life of its own. Through repetition one may reach a stage of boredom, of mechanical action, but later, it again becomes full of life. This renewal of interest comes because we can begin to see it from a new and more objective vantage-point, from which the actor is seen now to be contributing to an overall structure which is now in existence—and not just 'starting from scratch'. To reach this level of objective performance during the period of rehearsal is a very different matter, though.

First in both stage movement and stage speaking we must discover in greater detail the form that lies within gesture and the structure and form that lies within speaking. Much has been written and demonstrated on movement. Kinetic analyses, the work of Rudolf Laban, dance groups, mime companies and so on, all indicate a great enthusiasm for experiencing every kind of movement from free-style to ritualistic.

There is always an enthusiastic audience for dance and mime. Much has been written on this subject. We will go on now to consider the audio-kinetic sense (if I may so put it) that we possess, that allows us to appreciate movement in speech.

EXERCISE: MIMES FOR AUDIO-KINETIC SENSE

Choose a mood—such as thoughtful, anxious, tentative, determined—and in such a mood perform everyday actions, such as sorting papers, laying a table, preparing a meal. This is to experience an overall colouring of the action by a certain mood. The spectators can watch that the mood is maintained.

Next we can speak the lines set down below, to find a primary gesture for each line. This process can be helped by someone reading the line and the actor moving or even 'dancing' the line. The repetition in some of the lines is to help the actor when moving to find the gesture in these exclamations. Having moved a line he may then say the line transferring in his mind's eye his movement into the delivery of the line.

A Now, now, now, I begin to suspect that he does not speak the truth.

B I doubt it—I doubt it very much—I can't imagine that he would do it.

C Can't you see, can't you see how stubborn you are?

D I am amazed, amazed to hear you say such a thing!

E Never, never, never in a thousand years, would I agree to such a thing.

F Couldn't we try to reach—to reach some arrangement, come to—come to some agreement?

G For God's sake—can't you see what's happening, can't you understand? ▶

H Now it's all over—all finished—thank God for that!

I You know, I have a funny feeling that it is all going to be all right—it's going to be fine.

J I wish I could find a way out of this—I really do.

K Maybe he'll come back, maybe he'll return—and then be sorry and say that he's sorry, and then we'll all laugh and be glad.

CHAPTER 6
Discovery of Movement in Speech

In the sixteenth century, an actor could stand out on a thrust stage and create the drama solely by means of his gesture and speaking. We can recreate the experience of this by reading, say, the prayer speech of King Claudius in Hamlet. We can experience his search for security in his situation. This is shown both in the literal meaning of the lines and in the phrasing and dynamic shape of the sentences. These qualities can become apparent if the actor moves to the lines while they are read by someone else. This may be a slow and gentle process at first, but gradually the 'dance' quality of the speech becomes more obvious.

The point of this exercise is for the actor to bring the thoughts into movement. This simple exercise can provide the basis for much of our work.

When we read, what we are doing is to translate the words on the printed page into thoughts. Unless we soon transform the thoughts into *deeds*, by, say, moving or dancing the thoughts, they become over-attached to the 'head process'.

For example, if at some time you have had to think intensely about something, perhaps during a time of crisis, you may have found the need to pace up and down the room in order to drive the thoughts onwards to some conclusion. The activity of the will-power in pacing stimulates the action of thinking.

This may not happen all that often in private life, but when thoughts have to be declaimed they have to become *active*.

If it is not recognized in drama, then we will continue to get what so often happens today—an actor moving or gesticulating while a stream of static sentences pours from his lips. So long as we remain unaccustomed to expect anything else, this may not be so noticeable. But having paced and danced speeches and having heard the thoughts moving through the spoken words as though truly freed from the page of text, I have come to see this exercise as essential training.

Later on the actor, having familiarized himself with the lines, can perhaps pace the speech out in dumb show. This practice will freshen the dynamic of the speech, giving it that quality of moving forward to form the thought.

Finally, the speech can be delivered without showing outwardly the movement of the thought. The appearance will then be still, but the speaking will retain the movement of dance within it.

Our movements can sing just as our speech can dance.

Movement in Speaking: Gibberish

We can experience movement in speaking as a game. A group try to converse in gibberish, that is, a totally invented language they have created. The main object of the exercise is to hear the inflexion as we copy the cadence of speech without any content.

The expressive quality that lies within the inflected voice can be vastly entertaining for the speakers, as can the awareness that understanding comes not only from the literal meaning but also from the dynamic flow of the speech. In gibberish there is clearly no absolute meaning, yet expression abounds. You make a series of sounds, perhaps such as to appear that you are questioning someone. You pause as though for an answer. No answer comes, so you speak again, and this further gibberish phrase appears entirely out of your experience of your previous inflexions. A natural feeling for the rightness of the next expression arises.

As before, with movement, the sound gesture reflects itself in us, and we are able to bring another gesture forward in response.

Let us find the gesture or the dynamic in some lines of dialogue, in the same manner as with the gibberish. This time, however, we give some content to the sounds. The following few 'speech-dances' can be tried in four different ways:

1 With a partner reading, and the performer finding the shape of the sentence in *travelling* movement. I stress 'travelling' to do

battle with the notion that expression in speech is just a matter of moving up and down in pitch. By stepping, running, even jumping, we begin to feel that speaking also *travels*.

2 Saying it silently—like inner music—but outwardly moving to it.

3 Moving and speaking it with the changing dynamics carried out in *large* movements, the transitions from one dynamic to another being noted and outwardly expressed.

4 With the physical gesture coming first, the words following. The gesture can be small, and the speech apparently natural.

SPEECH-DANCES

Movement and sound dynamic

Now I understand, at last I've got it, I get it, and it's true, that is truth, I see it, I see it, what a great feeling it is to grasp an idea, to grab it, hold it . . . to get it. To keep it. What was it? What was it? I've lost it. What was it? Now, calm. Find it. Feel for it. That thought. It was a good one. It was a great thought . . . but what was it? Wait. No, it's gone. Gone. Well, we had a great time together, that thought and I, but now it's gone. Gone. I'm thought-jilted.

* * * * *

No, I will not stand for it! That is enough! It is enough! The worm turns. The dog must have his day. Begone dull care and let the devil take the hindmost. Yet how can you be brave when there seems to be nothing to be brave about? To be brave is to enjoy the feeling of resistance. Then I will resist. I will confront. I will oppose. Stand firm. Immovable. Implacable. Irreversible. In defeat indomitable. In victory insufferable. Magnificent. I would stamp my foot if those below wouldn't bang on their ceiling. Let them bang on their ceiling, I will stamp my foot. Dare I? Just once. Here goes. I stamp my foot! Now bang on your ceiling. Silence! I stamp my foot again. Nothing from below. (Bang from below.) Ah! you answer, do you? Then I stamp again. (Stamp, bang, stamp, bang.) I think that's enough. Now for some coffee.

*　*　*　*　*

Simple, so simple, divinely simple. Neat and perfect. So superbly simple. Not a wrinkle in it. Smooth, sleek, slick and . . . but why go on, I complicate its simplicity. Too glib? Too glib? Could that be levelled at it? Too slick, too chic? No, it had the smooth touch of a divine masseur. The mesmeric measure of a magician's mime. The sensitive gesture of the sleight-of-hand. Too smooth? Too smooth? Yes, perhaps too smooth by far.

*　*　*　*　*

From Hamlet, *Act III, Scene III*

KING. Oh! my offence is rank, it smells to Heaven;
   It hath the primal eldest curse upon't,
   A brother's murder! Pray can I not,
   Though inclination be as sharp as will:
   My stronger guilt defeats my strong intent,
   And, like a man to double business bound,
   I stand in pause where I shall first begin,
   And both neglect. What if this cursed hand
   Were thicker than itself with brother's blood,
   Is there no rain enough in the sweet heavens
   To wash it white as snow? Whereto serves mercy
   But to confront the visage of offence?
   And what's in prayer but this twofold force,
   To be forestalled, ere we come to fall,
   Or pardon'd being down? Then I'll look up;
   My fault is past. But O! what form of prayer
   Can serve my turn? 'Forgive me my foul murder'?
   That cannot be, since I am still possess'd
   Of those effects for which I did the murder,
   My crown, mine own ambition, and my queen.
   May one be pardon'd, and retain the offence?
   In the corrupted currents of this world,

68

Offence's gilded hand may shove by justice,
And oft 'tis seen the wicked prize itself
Buys out the law; but 'tis not so above;
There is no shuffling, there the action lies
In his true nature, and we ourselves compell'd
Even to the teeth and forehead of our faults,
To give evidence. What then? what rests?
Try what repentance can. What can it not?
Yet what can it, when one cannot repent?
O wretched state! O bosom black as death!
O limed soul, that, struggling to be free,
Art more engaged. Help, angels! make assay;
Bow, stubborn knees; and heart with strings of steel
Be soft as sinews of the new-born babe.
All may be well.

Replacing pitch with movement

I have already referred to the belief that expressiveness in speech relies only on the rise and fall of the voice. This indeed may appear to be so. However, in artistic speaking we can have an entirely different picture. Thus, if our voice rises in pitch the actor should imagine that it encompasses more space, as the voice falls in pitch less space. As with gesture, if you raise your arms above your head it is not only that you have raised your arms but your experience is of expanding; by bringing your arms down below the shoulder you perhaps feel that spatially you are surrounding yourself. If in speaking as in gesture we think more of expanding and contracting and less of the rising and falling of pitch we may come to a more imaginative approach to both gesture and speech.

CHAPTER 7
Six Attitudes in Gesture and Speech

If we reflect on our experience of the drama, we see there is a basic limitation on the scope of expression allowed us by our physical senses. As we only have a limited number of senses, so we only have a limited number of forms of basic expression.

In his lectures on speech and drama, Rudolf Steiner mentioned some basic attitudes which come to expression in distinctive gestures and voice tones.

First, there is the *effective* gesture, that gesture in which we 'accomplish something'. From it we derive the satisfaction which comes from having completed an action. This can be seen in sport, in which there is always a movement from effort to a conclusion—striking a ball, throwing a spear, shooting an arrow, winning a race, hurling a discus. The ultimate satisfaction in sport is to do something *effectively*. This satisfaction can, to a limited extent, be obtained passively, or vicariously—say in reading an 'action-packed' novel.

But the sportsman's or the novel-reader's experience is only a dim shadow of the *movement* possible in every kind of human activity. Every human being has in some degree the impulse to 'do' something, whether in physical action or in thought, in ideas or in conversation. The 'talent to organize' is one example; 'active sympathy' can be another.

The gesture indicating the presence of this human impulse is outward-going—pointing, commanding and giving orders, emphatically tapping a table to make a point, speaking in ringing tones, as in persuasive oratory. Every action or speech by an actor needs something of this gesture; however timid, weak or vacillating the character portrayed may be, there is still this underlying aspect of 'effectiveness'.

A second gesture is that of *sympathy*, carrying with it a quality of 'opening oneself' to the event confronting us, such as a person or situation. To expand beyond one's own defences becomes increasingly difficult to achieve today. The world presses in upon us in many ways, stunting our sympathy, creating a too protective attitude. On the other hand, a general sympathy has grown to world proportions. There are those who feel for and indeed fight for the weaker sections in society; they are to be found in such work as animal care and refugee relief. So where our more immediate sympathies may be stunted in some way, due to our own anxiety, a greater and deeply responsible sympathy for the world has spread. This outward-going 'opening' quality appears as a surrounding gesture, a gentle touching of the object that has aroused sympathy and a gentleness in speaking.

The third outgoing gesture can be described as a 'striving forward against hindrances'. This may be the noblest gesture. In its attitude of questioning, searching, seeking—and discovering—it indicates that most positive element in human nature, the urge to progress. 'Woe betide him who does not ask, who does not question.' In this gesture we feel forward with the hands, pressing onwards, perhaps carefully or diplomatically, perhaps aggressively, perhaps youthfully, discovering life and ourselves in the process.

The chorus in Greek classical drama would enquire, with a trembling or vibrating voice, into the rights and wrongs of the action before them—debating, deciding, continually seeking the right path, leading onward through conflict. This could not but arouse in the listener a sense of pressing forward in spite of doubt and fear. Much of *Hamlet* expresses this sense.

The remaining three gestures are opposite to the first three, being retiring, contracting and affirming, as opposed to expanding, opening out or penetrating into the world.

The opposite to 'effective' could be the inner attitude *thoughtful*. The outer attitude of 'thoughtful' is easily recognized and would appear to have a restraining quality, as though one is holding onself in check. Pressing the fingertips together, holding one's head, stroking one's chin, pinching one's nose or ear-lobe, standing with hands on hips, or even assuming something of the posture of Rodin's *The Thinker*—all these involve something of restraint—the opposite to the pointing gesture of 'effective'. It is as though a man has to restrain a certain outward-going action in order to allow the inner activity of thought to work in him. In sport one can see the two gestures working together, first thoughtful preparation and then the change of attitude from thought to deed, as the athlete first prepares, and then flings himself into action. The contrast is more noticeable the more expert the athlete.

This taking hold of oneself in order to allow the inner activity of thought to work freely is most impressive as a gesture; with it, the speech becomes measured and full in tone. Now here is an interesting point: how often nowadays do we see an actor thinking aloud on the stage, creating a pattern of thought before our eyes and ears?

Of course, one hears the *results* of thought expressed often enough. What I am talking about is the *actual process of thinking*, in which, if we saw it, we would be following the *development* of concepts towards a completely resolved thought-form.

In English drama the trial scene has always been popular, ever since the court scene in *The Merchant of Venice*. This contains drama in the exchange of thoughts. It can be very satisfying, because one comes near to following a train of thought leading to a form of resolution, even though what is said is only the *results* of thinking which, in the court circumstances, has to be very rapid.

If we can project the thoughts themselves being unravelled, creating a kind of meditative drama, this may deepen the satisfaction (see Rudolf Steiner's four Mystery plays).

Our next gesture, the *antipathetic*, contrasts with our outgoing sympathy. It is really a form of withdrawing from a situation, person or object, but instead of retiring from it we push away what antagonizes us. We push or fling something away or, in certain circumstances, fling *ourselves* away from what we reject, as in leaving the room, flinging oneself out of the house, and so on. At first glance this would seem an obvious reaction, yet it conveys itself often in a most subtle way. To step back and critically observe something is antipathetic. Likewise any show of resistance has antipathy in it. To be courageous has antipathy within it. Antipathy is not necessarily only negative. To withstand the impressions of city life often demands antipathy from us as a defence. Indeed I suspect that much of daily life arouses subconscious antipathy within us, as a protection against it. The human being has the ability not to hear sounds, either because of familiarity with the sound or because something interests us more; and also not to see even something as challenging as a poster if we shut our mind to it. To ignore impressions all around us is to arouse an antipathy towards them. One could not travel in an underground train if one were wholly sympathetic to what came to meet you as impressions. For many of us antipathy has become a necessity. Deep within the human soul is the longing to express sympathy; but there is also the need to find strength in antipathy. When working with an actor who has not yet fully conveyed his character, I have found that 'seasoning' his work with a feeling of antipathy can clarify—give definition to—the performance.

The sixth gesture can be described as 'withdrawing onto one's own ground'. This attitude complements the 'feeling forward' gesture that rapidly shifts between two phases, between going out and closing inward. This sixth gesture neither repulses nor encourages an outer experience but allows the sense of self to dominate the surroundings.

An example can be seen on any crowded bus or train. We stand pressed against each other in some closed compartment, yet we remain curiously aloof from the situation, each of us our own island. The Greek statue, the *Charioteer*, has this quality; column-like he stands, calmly holding the reins. Within this gesture is the *observer* who can survey events around him and arrive at his own conclusions.

In studying these six gestures it is important to be aware not only of the superficial appearance, of the trivialities, of the behaviour in question. Equally it must be grasped that between them they contain every nuance of action of the human being in the world. With these six attitudes, every form of penetrating the world, every mode of receiving impressions from the world, can be covered. For the actor, if he is aware of this universal quality in his every gesture, this can become a basis for his art.

These brief notes should not be seen as attempting more than a rough sketch of these six gestures. To try to do more would only burden the reader with preconceptions and get in the way of his own unprejudiced observation of the human actions around him. I hope the examples given may, however, serve as a guide towards independent research by the reader into the deeper significance of these expressions of the human soul.

Exercises in the Six Basic Gestures

Effective and thoughtful

For the effective gesture, actors carry out a sequence which involves hurried searching. They could be soldiers feverishly trying to find some documents. They look in one place, and then move to the next possible hiding place. There is little thought, but a great deal of action.

Gradually, as they fail to find the documents, they become more *thoughtful*. The emphasis of the action becomes more on pondering and looking around rather than on the action of searching. Finally, the action may stop altogether, the actors only thoughtfully looking about the room and only after much thinking move with decision to a likely hiding place. So in this simple drama we have moved from effectiveness to thinking, back to effective movement. The action should end with the discovery of the documents, to provide a feeling of satisfaction at accomplishing what they had set out to do. Next we can repeat this scene, but with the careful use of 'gibberish' in order to bring the sound gesture into the sequence. The *effective* speaking should be somewhat quick and metallic, the thoughtful discussion in the middle of the piece slow and full-toned, and the sequence then ends with mostly determined and incisive sounds.

Sympathy and antipathy

This can be acted in a scene which begins when a man dies from some contest or street fight. The group gather round him, uncertain what to do.

Then they see a relative of the dead man approaching, a brother

74

or a sister. They rush to prevent the relative from coming near, but the relative, sensing something is wrong, pushes the protesting group aside, strongly, one by one. The feeling of rejection or antipathy can be helped by the actors falling away from the approaching brother or sister more easily than would be the case in real life. This helps the approaching character to get a strong feeling of effective antipathy.

Suddenly he or she stands in front of the dead brother and immediately reverses his expression to one of deep sympathy. The group stand around in a passive, sympathetic circle as the relative looks at the dead man. The group then drift slowly away.

Again, speech or gibberish can be added to the scene to bring the gesture into sound expression.

Feeling forward against hindrances

A mime similar to the tractor mime used earlier (p. 60) is helpful. We approach something with uncertainty and a feeling of tension, since we are *questioning*.

For example, using some simple objects lying to hand, like some chairs, one can build a sort of 'Stonehenge' effect. The actors come to these objects and study them, trying to penetrate their mystery. You can sometimes see this 'feeling forward' gesture in museums, when visitors gaze at, say, Egyptian statues, puzzled, but inwardly seeking to penetrate the purpose of such structures. The sequence can end, in this case rather unsatisfactorily, as the actors drift away, gazing back every so often in the earnest attempt to understand these lonely objects.

Another sequence can be the story of Pandora and the box. Her parents having left the palace, she decides to open the box that has been forbidden her. She enters the room, comes near to the box, feels for the secret catch to open it. Her hesitancy, her guilt, her fear of being discovered, together with her driving curiosity, combine to create the inner tensions of this gesture.

Here the performer can whisper her thoughts as she approaches the box, bringing the gesture quite naturally into her speaking.

Withdrawing onto one's own ground

This can be experienced by acting out a scene of a tourist visiting an Arabian bazaar. The merchants, played by the others in the group, fling themselves on the visitor with much pushing and imploring, cajoling and begging in full voice. The purpose could be to intimidate the actor who is playing the visitor. He, however, must move through them, calmly rejecting their offers with firm words and gesture. Finally, the merchants retire, defeated by the inner strength of the visitor.

Duologues on the Six Gestures

Effective and thoughtful

Effective **A**
> Stop it! Don't try it on! Just cut it out! Enough is enough! I warn you, if you try once again to persuade people against my better judgement, I'll do you an injury. So watch it—and stop it!

Thoughtful **B**
> Oh, now for heavens sake, what an attitude to take. Let's use a bit of thought, shall we? Let's think this through. Time is on our side. There is room for discussion. I have no wish to persuade. When I think back, what I was trying to do was see the situation from all sides, trying to see every aspect of the case.

A Then don't! That isn't what is required. You must grasp the situation, clearly and firmly, and make an instant decision. This is the art of active living. Grab the nettle before it can sting!

B No, no. On the contrary, you must approach the nettle, if you so wish to use such a metaphor, with caution, consider this and that, the pros and cons, consider every . . .

A I've no time for such meanderings. Grasp the situation firmly and decide . . .

B You won't even listen to what I'm saying . . .

A You take too long!

B You are too impetuous. You attack ideas, not create them, you force events, not shape them. You stamp your mark on life rather than offer suggestions, which gives the impression sometimes of thoughtless action.

A You are all think and no do. I weary of you!

B I fear for you.

Sympathy and antipathy gestures

A Oh, what a beautiful painting!

B Cheap rubbish!

A The delicate colouring conjures a fresh world of dreams before the vision.

B Childish daubing. It should not have been displayed.

A Then what is this one? A gentle pastoral scene lovingly depicted.

B Sentimental realism. A photograph could have done better—though I hate photographs.

A But doesn't it awake memories of childhood, of peace, of days of calm?

B You are a pitiful ass. Your critical faculties are non-existent. Your judgements have all the effectiveness of a damp sponge.

A I admire your certainty, but I suspect it is only possible, such certainty, when it refuses to let impressions work upon it.

B Nonsense, my impression of you has worked upon me.

A I understand how you feel.

B You don't. Goodbye.

A Your leaving like that is sad.

Feeling forward and withdrawing gestures

A Is there no way in which we can reconcile our differences?

B No. If there was, there would be no need to ask the question.

A I cannot believe that our association has finally reached its conclusion.

B I not only believe it but am determined that it shall be so.

A Let us try once again to find a way to resolve these misunderstandings.

B Do leave me alone.

A I am serious.

B So am I.

A I'm trying to find a way out of this situation.

B There is no way out.

A It's too stupid.

B Agreed.

A It's too easy.

B Nothing is too easy.

A You're not being helpful.

B That's true.

A Then I must leave.

B [*remains silent*].

CHAPTER 8
The Sense of Rhythm, and Dynamic Speaking

Where is the heartbeat of acting? We have our own rhythmic system—our heartbeat and our breathing rhythm. The sense of rhythm in the body guides our sense of timing and proportion in our acting. The ancient story-tellers, the speakers of epic, based their delivery on the metric form known as the hexameter. This rhythm was believed to reflect the ratio between heartbeat and breath, i.e. four heartbeats to one breath. Walter Johannes Stein, in his book *Labour*, describes this theory.

> In the normal way we breathe 18 times a minute, during which period the pulse registers 72 beats; that is to say, our pulse beats four times during each breath we take. This relationship of 1 to 4 is, however, a cosmic relationship. We draw our breath 25,920 times in a day and this number multiplied by 4, giving the number 103,681, represents the daily number of heartbeats. These are heavenly numbers. The rhythm of the precession of the equinox and the rhythms of the apogee and perigee correspond to these numbers.
>
> In olden days song was the perfectly natural accompaniment of work—song founded on the rhythm of metrical speech. But verse itself has its origin, as Rudolf Steiner has shown, in the relationship of the rhythms of blood and breathing. Thus, for example, the Greek hexameter is based on the rhythm of one to four. The hexameter has one pause in the middle of the line and another at the end. If we count these pauses, which are equal to one foot in duration, also as feet, then it is clear that the hexameter consists not of six feet, but of eight; twice four feet

gives a hexameter. This corresponds to two indrawn breaths and 2 × 4 pulse beats. Therefore, we see that this ancient measure of verse is derived from the harmonic relationship of blood and breath.

By regularly speaking verses in hexameters, and sometimes stepping the rhythm, a feeling for the actor's inner decision and sense of rhythm is heightened in a particularly subtle way. We will come back to the hexameter again in Chapter 11, pp.131–3.

THE HEXAMETER

Speech is a gift to mankind, | and by speech is community founded. |
Man is companion to man | by the sharing of joy and disaster. |
Who has not known of anxiety | lightened by nearness of friendship? |
Who has not known glad days | brightened by sharing of pleasure? |
How many wonderful deeds, | the result of man's council together, |
Live in the songs of the bards, | whose words are the cradle of history? |
Poets inspire us with beauty, | in sound, form, colour and image, |
Winging words to the ears, | to the hearts of the one that can love them. |
Speak then the speech of mankind, | and give glory to God and his angels. |

Barbara Bridgmont

Sometimes our innate sense of rhythm needs to be reawakened, in which case the following exercise is useful.

A group stands in a circle and one person begins to stamp her feet and clap her hands while dancing inside the circle. She throws the rhythm to another member of the group who collects that rhythm and either continues with it or changes it as he or she wishes. Having established a rhythmic pattern we throw it to someone else as though it were a conversation. This continues until all have had a turn. We begin again but reduce the stamping and clapping to the minimum, the sense of rhythm living in the silence. Finally, the first person begins again but with no stamping or clapping at all, only silent movement which she passes on. We can now separate into partners and each in turn move as though holding a conversation, and so it goes backwards and forwards, a duologue of dance. The next stage is to take this sense of the dynamic into speaking by doing a sketch or improvisation, or by reading the duologue below.

CHANGING DYNAMIC IN SPEECH AND GESTURE

A Hello, I do apologize, so sorry I'm late. I got caught up in the traffic.

B I don't want to hear your excuses, you're late and I have been waiting here for over a quarter of an hour.

A Look, I apologized, didn't I? I said I was sorry . . .

B That's not good enough. To say you are sorry doesn't disguise the fact that I have been waiting here for a quarter of an hour.

A Well, try to forget and forgive, and let's plan our evening.

B It's spoilt already.

A Nonsense!

B It is *not* nonsense. Don't think that you can blithely pass over the fact that . . .

A I can't believe this! Are you always like this when things go a little wrong, obsessive and stupid?

B Oh, no! That is the cruellest thing that has ever been said to me. That is wicked, vile and sadistic.

A Please, I'm sorry. I didn't mean to upset you. I'm afraid I was just showing off, you know, being smart, saying clever things.

81

B	How can you say I'm obsessive! How can you say things like that! I'm not, I'm not. I never have been . . .
A	All right, all right. Keep calm. Please forget what I've said and let's plan the evening.
B	Yes, yes. That's just like you, always wishing to forget—forget that you were late, forget that you were rude and hurtful. What else have you forgotten?
A	I'll never forget *you*, that's for sure.
B	I wonder, I wonder. Perhaps you daren't try and remember all your friends, your enemies, all the things you've said, all the horrible things you've said, the hurtful cruel . . .
A	Listen, listen. Can you hear something?
B	No.
A	Neither can I. Sorry, it was the only way I could think of making you stop.
B	Oh, you are so cruel.
A	Yes, yes.
B	Also you are short.
A	Short?
B	Yes, short. Now I come to look at you.
A	I'm not short.
B	Yes you are.
A	If you say that again I'll walk away. I'll leave you.
B	I won't cry.
A	I'm not short. I'm definitely not short. You're the first person to say that I'm short, the very first person. Nobody has ever said I'm short, nobody.
B	Have you finished?

A	Yes.
B	Now we've both been hurt, and I'm sorry.
A	Sorry isn't good enough.
B	It will have to do. I'm sorry.
A	You're getting your own back on me.
B	Yes. You were late.
A	I'm sorry—but I'm not short.
B	No, sorry.
A	I was late, but I'm not short.
B	No, I mean, yes.
A	I'm sorry that I was late.
B	And I'm sorry that you are short.
A	I'm hungry.
B	So am I.
A	Then let's go for a meal.
B	Let's.

The following scene from Shakespeare's *Macbeth* will further illustrate the timing of dynamic speaking.

MACBETH, ACT II, SCENE II

[Enter Lady Macbeth]

LADY M. That which hath made them drunk hath made me
    bold;
  What hath quench'd them hath given me fire.
  Hark! Peace!
  It was the owl that shriek'd, the fatal bellman,
  Which gives the stern'st good-night. He is about it:
  The doors are open, and the surfeited grooms
  Do mock their charge with snores: I have drugg'd their possets,
  That Death and Nature do contend about them,
  Whether they live or die.

MACBETH [*within*] Who's there? what, ho!

LADY M. Alack! I am afraid they have awak'd,
And 'tis not done. The attempt and not the deed
Confounds us. Hark! I laid their daggers ready;
He could not miss 'em. Had he not resembled
My father as he slept, I had done't. My husband!

[*Enter Macbeth*]

MACBETH. I have done the deed. Didst thou not hear a noise?

LADY M. I heard the owl scream and the crickets cry.
Did not you speak?

MACBETH. When?

LADY M. Now.

MACBETH. As I descended?

LADY M. Ay.

MACBETH. Hark!
Who lies i' the second chamber?

LADY M. Donalbain.

MACBETH. [*Looking at his hands*] This is a sorry sight.

LADY M. A foolish thought, to say a sorry sight.

MACBETH. There's one did laugh in's sleep, and one cried
'Murder!'
That they did wake each other: I stood and heard them;
But they did say their prayers, and address'd them
Again to sleep.

LADY M. There are two lodg'd together.

MACBETH. One cried 'God bless us!' and 'Amen,' the other;
As they had seen me with these hangman's hands.
List'ning their fear, I could not say 'Amen,'
When they did say 'God bless us!'

LADY M. Consider it not so deeply.

MACBETH. But wherefore could not I pronounce 'Amen'?
I had most need of blessing, and 'Amen'
Stuck in my throat.

LADY M. These deeds must not be thought
After these ways; so, it will make us mad.

MACBETH. Methought I heard a voice cry 'Sleep no more!
Macbeth does murder sleep,' the innocent sleep,
Sleep that knits up the ravell'd sleave of care,
The death of each day's life, sore labour's bath,
Balm of hurt minds, great nature's second course,
Chief nourisher in life's feast—

LADY M. What do you mean?

MACBETH. Still it cried 'Sleep no more!' to all the house:
'Glamis hath murder'd sleep, and therefore Cawdor
Shall sleep no more, Macbeth shall sleep no more!

LADY M. Who was it that thus cried? Why, worthy thane,
You do unbend your noble strength, to think
So brainsickly of things. Go get some water,
And wash this filthy witness from your hand.
Why did you bring these daggers from the place?
They must lie there: go carry them, and smear
The sleepy grooms with blood.

MACBETH. I'll go no more:
I am afraid to think what I have done;
Look on't again I dare not.

LADY M. Infirm of purpose!
Give me the daggers. The sleeping and the dead
Are but as pictures; 'tis the eye of childhood
That fears a painted devil. If he do bleed,
I'll gild the faces of the grooms withal;
For it must seem their guilt. [*Exit. Knocking within*]

MACBETH. Whence is that knocking?
How is't with me, when every noise appals me?
What hands are here? Ha! they pluck out mine eyes.
Will all great Neptune's ocean wash this blood

Clean from my hand? No, this my hand will rather
The multitudinous seas incarnadine,
Making the green one red.
[Re-enter Lady Macbeth]

LADY M. My hands are of your colour; but I shame
To wear a heart so white. [Knocking within] I hear a knocking
At the south entry: retire we to our chamber;
A little water clears us of this deed:
How easy is it, then! Your constancy
Hath left you unattended. [Knocking within] Hark! more
knocking.
Get on your nightgown, lest occasion call us,
And show us to be watchers. Be not lost
So poorly in your thoughts.
MACBETH. To know my deed, 'twere best not know myself.
[Knocking within]
Wake Duncan with thy knocking! I would thou couldst!

[Exeunt]

Wrestling in Action and Speech

We know that one of the ancient Greek gymnastics was wrestling.
By wrestling we extend a sense of gesture beyond the physical
limitations. We try wrestling, and then jump apart and continue
wrestling across the space between the partners, conversing with
gestures in the space across the stage, gradually moving further
apart and then coming together again. We grip our opponent, and
this reminds us that performers must be united across the stage in
spirit if not in practice. The next stage is to take the wrestling into
the dynamic of speaking; for this I have included a short scene as
an exercise, followed by part of Act I, Scene I from Shakespeare's
Richard III.

WRESTLING INTO DUOLOGUE

A Why don't you do as I say?

B Because there is not reason to.

A There is every reason, if you think carefully.

B Why bother to think carefully; I can feel that it would be better to leave things as they are.

A No! Sometimes you make me so angry!

B I make *you* angry! I sometimes wonder why I ever talk to you.

A All right, all right. Let's start again. Unless I write to him and explain, he'll never understand.

B He doesn't need to. It doesn't matter what he thinks.

A It does!

B No. What he thinks doesn't change the situation.

A True, but out of common decency we should inform him how we came to our decision.

B What's the point!

A Never mind the point, let's write to him.

B All right. If you have nothing better to do, by all means write.

A I have a lot of things better to do but I'm trying to help an awkward situation.

B Created by yourself.

A It was not!

B It was!

[*Silence*]

A I will write to him.

B No, I will.

A You'll just be insulting.

B No I won't. I'll be gentle.

A Promise!

B Yes.

A Let's shake on that.

B Let's.

[They shake hands.]

FROM *RICHARD III*, ACT I, SCENE II

GLOUCESTER. Lady, you know no rules of charity,
  Which renders good for bad, blessings for curses.

ANNE. Villain, thou know'st no law of God nor man:
  No beast so fierce but knows some touch of pity.

GLOUCESTER. But I know none, and therefore am no beast.

ANNE. O wonderful, when devils tell the truth!

GLOUCESTER. More wonderful, when angels are so angry.
  Vouchsafe, divine perfection of a woman,
  Of these supposed evils, to give me leave
  By circumstance, but to acquit myself.

ANNE. Vouchsafe, diffused infection of a man,
  For these known evils, but to give me leave
  By circumstance, to curse thy cursed self.

GLOUCESTER. Fairer than tongue can name thee, let me have
  Some patient leisure to excuse myself.

ANNE. Fouler than heart can think thee, thou canst make
  No excuse current, but to hang thyself.

GLOUCESTER. By such despair, I should accuse myself.

ANNE. And, by despairing, shalt thou stand excused
  For doing worthy vengeance on thyself,
  Which didst unworthy slaughter upon others.

GLOUCESTER. Say that I slew them not?

ANNE. Then say they were not slain:
  But dead they are, and, devilish slave, by thee.

GLOUCESTER. I did not kill your husband.

ANNE. Why, then he is alive.

GLOUCESTER. Nay, he is dead; and slain by Edward's hand.

ANNE. In thy foul throat thou liest: Queen Margaret saw
    Thy murderous falchion smoking in his blood;
    The which thou once didst bend against her breast,
    But that thy brothers beat aside the point.

GLOUCESTER. I was provoked by her slanderous tongue,
    That laid their guilt upon my guiltless shoulders.

ANNE. Thou wast provoked by thy bloody mind,
    That never dreamt on aught but butcheries.
    Didst thou not kill this king?

GLOUCESTER. I grant ye.

ANNE. Dost grant me, hedgehog? Then God grant me too
    Thou mayst be damned for that wicked deed!
    O, he was gentle, mild, and virtuous!

GLOUCESTER. The fitter for the King of heaven, that hath
    him.

ANNE. He is in heaven, where thou shalt never come.

GLOUCESTER. Let him thank me, that help to send him
    thither;
    For he was fitter for that place than earth.

ANNE. And thou unfit for any place but hell.

GLOUCESTER. Yes, one place else, if you will hear me name it.

ANNE. Some dungeon.

RICHARD. Your bed-chamber.

Attraction, Repulsion

As part of the training to familiarize ourselves with living beyond
our physical boundaries, consider the power of attraction. What
we desire draws us like a magnet, as though an outer force has
power over us. Conversely, when we are repulsed by something
it is as though it pushes us away; we run from the image, real or

imaginary, that haunts us. If we see someone in the street whom we wish to meet, the way they walk and talk attracts us. The opposite can be the case with those we wish to avoid; their image repulses us.

In the game of attraction/repulsion we imagine we enter a temple as thieves. There, at the end of the building, is a statue holding jewels but, as we approach, we fear the temple and the statue and yet we are urged on by our greed. Still we draw back from the mystery and hidden danger which seems present. The sense of being pulled by the jewels or being pushed away by the invisible threat reminds us how much we live outside ourselves, although we may be unaware of this in everyday life. For drama, however, an essential quality in our acting is that we live outside ourselves in the world of attraction and withdrawing. Although we are speaking of invisible activity, the audience develops a sense for it. I have presented the two qualities, attraction and repulsion, in a brief scene as an exercise in speech dynamics. Following it is a similar exercise taken from a scene in *Romeo and Juliet*.

ATTRACTION/REPULSION

A [*looking for something in a desk*]

B [*enters*] Is this what you are looking for? [*holding out a brooch*]

A Oh yes. Why have you got it?

B Well, I did originally give it to you. So in a way it's mine.

A What a charming thought. Is that how you usually consider gifts?

B Please, don't let's argue.

A I was actually looking for the brooch in order to give it back to you.

B How fortunate that I took it first; it has saved you the trouble and embarrassment of returning it to me.

A That's true, for which I am grateful.

B You know its value, of course?

A Surely you mean its price?

B Do you know its price?

A No, and I don't wish to, as it has no value for me now.

B If you knew its price, you would see that the gift was of great value, in every sense of the word.

A Even so, that gift cost too much. Through that brooch, you tried to dominate me, control me and run my life as if it belonged to you. The cost of the brooch was too high.

B Particularly now, when it would seem that its receiver was so low.

A Words . . . words . . . that is all we have left, and they break no bones. I am relieved that the exchange of words and gifts is now over and I'm free to go.

B What gifts have we exchanged? I have received nothing from you.

A My company may have seemed to you as nothing, but for me it was in the nature of a gift. A gift which at one time I was happy to give, but a gift ceases to be one when the recipient takes and takes. Now, I want my own soul back, thank you. If you'll excuse me, I'll leave.

B Not before I upbraid you for your selfishness, greed and patronizing manner.

A Just move out of my way and let me pass.

B No. And I'm going to keep this brooch . . .

A Do that . . .

B It possesses more value to me than your cheap soul.

A Keep it, but let me go.

B This brooch has a certain beauty, as well as a worldly value. It won't perish; it is loyal and true to the owner, never changing . . .

A Hard, lifeless carbon. Now let me go!

B All right, I'm not stopping you. I leave that to your conscience.

A [*snatching brooch*] But I'll take this with me.

[*Exit A*]

FROM *ROMEO AND JULIET*, ACT III, SCENE II, BY WILLIAM SHAKESPEARE

JULIET. O, here comes my nurse,
And she brings news; and every tongue that speaks
But Romeo's name speaks heavenly eloquence.
[*Enter nurse with cords*]
Now, nurse, what news? What hast thou there? the cords
That Romeo bid thee fetch?

NURSE. Ay, ay, the cords. [*Throwing them down*]

JULIET. Ay me! what news? why dost thou wring thy hands?

NURSE. Ay, well-a-day! he's dead, he's dead, he's dead!
We are undone, lady, we are undone!
Alack the day! he's gone, he's kill'd, he's dead!

JULIET. Can heaven be so envious?

NURSE. Romeo can,
Though heaven cannot: O Romeo, Romeo!
Who ever would have thought it? Romeo!

JULIET. What devil art thou, that dost torment me thus?
This torture should be roar'd in dismal hell.
Hath Romeo slain himself? say thou but 'I'.
And that bare vowel 'I' shall poison more
Than the death-darting eye of cockatrice:
I am not I, if there be such an I;
Or those eyes shut, that make thee answer 'I'.
If he be slain, say 'I'; or if not, no:
Brief sounds determine of my weal or woe.

NURSE. I saw the wound, I saw it with mine eyes—
God save the mark!—here on his manly breast:
A piteous corse, a bloody piteous corse;

92

Pale, pale as ashes, all bedaub'd in blood,
All in gore-blood: I swounded at the sight.

JULIET: O break, my heart! poor bankrupt, break at once!
To prison, eyes, ne'er look on liberty!
Vile earth, to earth resign; and motion here;
And thou and Romeo press one heavy bier!

NURSE. O Tybalt! Tybalt, the best friend I had!
O courteous Tybalt! honest gentleman!
That ever I should live to see thee dead!

JULIET. What storm is this that blows so contrary?
Is Romeo slaughter'd, and is Tybalt dead?
My dear-loved cousin, and my dearer lord?
Then, dreadful trumpet, sound the general doom!
For who is living, if those two are gone?

NURSE. Tybalt is gone, and Romeo banished;
Romeo that kill'd him, he is banished.

JULIET. O God! did Romeo's hand shed Tybalt's blood?

NURSE. It did, it did; alas the day, it did!

JULIET. O serpent heart, hid with a flowering face!
Did ever dragon keep so fair a cave?
Beautiful tyrant! friend angelical!
Dove-feather'd raven! wolvish-ravening lamb!
Despised substance of divinest show!
Just opposite to what thou justly seem'st,
A damned saint, an honourable villain!
O nature, what hadst thou to do in hell,
When thou didst bower the spirit of a fiend
In mortal paradise of such sweet flesh?
Was ever book containing such vile matter
So fairly bound? O, that deceit should dwell
In such a gorgeous palace!

NURSE. There's no trust,
No faith, no honesty in men; all perjured,
All forsworn, all naught, all dissemblers.
Ah, where's my man? give me some aqua vitae:

These griefs, these woes, these sorrows make me old.
Shame come to Romeo!

JULIET. Blister'd be thy tongue,
    For such a wish! he was not born to shame:
    Upon his brow shame is ashamed to sit;
    For 'tis a throne where honour may be crown'd
    Sole monarch of the universal earth.
    O, what a beast was I to chide at him!

NURSE. Will you speak well of him that kill'd your cousin?

JULIET. Shall I speak ill of him that is my husband?
    Ah, poor my lord, what tongue shall smooth thy name,
    When I, thy three-hours wife, have mangled it?
    But, wherefore, villain, didst thou kill my cousin?
    That villain cousin would have kill'd my husband:
    Back, foolish tears, back to your native spring;
    Your tributary drops belong to woe,
    Which you, mistaking, offer up to joy.
    My husband lives, that Tybalt would have slain;
    And Tybalt's dead, that would have slain my husband:
    All this is comfort; wherefore weep I then?
    Some word there was, worser than Tybalt's death,
    That murder'd me: I would forget it fain;
    But, O, it presses to my memory,
    Like damned guilty deeds to sinners' minds:
    'Tybalt is dead, and Romeo—banished';
    That 'banished', that one word 'banished',
    Hath slain ten thousand Tybalts. Tybalt's death
    Was woe enough, if it had ended there:
    Or, if sour woe delights in fellowship
    And needly will be rank'd with other griefs,
    Why follow'd not, when she said 'Tybalt's dead,'
    Thy father, or thy mother, nay, or both,
    Which modern lamentation might have moved?
    But with a rearward following Tybalt's death,
    'Romeo is banished', to speak that word,
    Is father, mother, Tybalt, Romeo, Juliet,
    All slain, all dead. 'Romeo is banished!'

There is no end, no limit, measure, bound,
In that word's death; no words can that woe sound.
Where is my father, and my mother, nurse?

NURSE. Weeping and wailing over Tybalt's corse:
Will you go to them? I will bring you thither.

JULIET. Wash they his wounds with tears: mine shall be spent,
When theirs are dry, for Romeo's banishment.
Take up those cords: poor ropes, you are beguiled,
Both you and I; for Romeo is exiled:
He made you for a highway to my bed;
But I, a maid, die maiden-widowed.
Come, cords, come, nurse; I'll to my wedding-bed;
And death, not Romeo, take my maidenhead!

NURSE. Hie to your chamber; I'll find Romeo
To comfort you: I wot well where he is.
Hark ye, your Romeo will be here at night:
I'll to him; he is hid at Laurence' cell.

JULIET. O, find him! give this ring to my true knight,
And bid him come to take his last farewell.

[Exeunt]

CHAPTER 9
Sound and Sense

The theatre building contains a bubble of air to be activated by the actor's speech.

Can we imagine that all sounds we utter are, in varying degrees, exclamations created by our inner reactions to outer events? One might say that they are in some respects descriptions of the events themselves. In ancient times, what was described in the word 'fire' was not only a reaction to the fire but a kind of description of the fire itself in the opening consonant 'F'. In speech men relived the experience of the fire; they were then not so much close to nature as somehow a part of it, closer than modern urban man can conceive. They possessed the unique quality of not only experiencing the living force within nature but of being able to express the activity of that force in dance and sound.

This can help us sense the depths from which speech springs. As human beings, we are able to relive an experience through sound and gesture, and pass it on to others. Through human sound, that has the ability to describe events and things, we can prove that men are not the result of a mere evolutionary process but beings possessed of spirit. Although deeply embedded in nature, human consciousness has set them apart from nature, allowing them to describe it—and themselves as well.

This ability of man to articulate a series of sounds far beyond the animal must set him apart from the animal. One of the distinguishing characteristics between animal and man is that man can speak. Indeed, human speech is a divine gift. If we were to lose consciousness of speech, if it were to become merely a mechanical communicating instrument or were to return to wild utterances (popular in a musical form today), and the essential

nature and gesture of speech were to become either misunder-
stood or lost, we would lose our divinity, our culture, our very
spirit.

The breath blows across the tongue, teeth, lips, palate, and
releases into the still air the forms and shapes of consonants and
vowels. The consonants, for instance, are created on the stream of
breath by the breath pressing past the various resistances set up
by the speech instruments within the mouth—the teeth with the
's' sound, the lips, with the 'b' sound, the teeth and lower lip with
the 'v' sound, the pressure of the tongue behind the teeth for the
'n' sound and so forth.

The sense of position in the mouth for releasing the vowel
sounds is of vital importance—the open mouth for the 'ah' sound,
the shift of focus forward when we speak the 'ae' sound (German
'ae' as in English 'sell'), the further shift forward between the
teeth for the 'ee' sound, the shaping of the 'o' with the lips as the
sound appears to fly out before us and the forward sound of the
'oo' through the pursed lips.

But for the speaker, such a mechanical description of the
creation of human sounds is not enough. The sound is evoked by
the speaker just as the javelin thrower we have previously
discussed allows energy to stream through his backward-reaching
arm. The breath is prepared, the speech organs are prepared, and
then, we imagine, the impulse for the human being to speak
comes from a different world.

The human being has the ability to shape a home for many
sounds. In fact in ancient times it was believed that these sounds
were the music of the planets and stars. Man has this ability but
is not the absolute creator of the sound itself.

Such discussions must be for another time and another book,
but the feeling of approaching sound, coming from our intention,
and the appearance of that sound, does so much towards bringing
a lively spirit to speaking in drama. In the book of Genesis, we are
referred to as clay or mineral into which life is breathed.
Something of this spirit always lies in the activity of artists.

Listening to Human Sounds

Within each sound, there is a quality of expression which is reflected in 'words'. It is as if there were gestures in both vowels and consonants; these can only be experienced, let alone understood, if listened to in the right way.

The right way to listen can be discovered if we imagine that the whole body is an instrument for listening—as if one receives the sound as a total experience. This may seem a strange way of looking at it. Listening to poetry or drama today, the speaking rarely possesses the sort of quality needed for that. But if we are listening to music it is quite easy to conceive of receiving a total bodily experience, and that it is not enough to cock one's head to one side and listen only with the ear.

If speaking can become more of a musical art, sensitive to the substance of speech, to the vowels and consonants, we will then find listening to human speech to be a deeper experience, rather like the experience of listening to music.

If words are the messengers of our minds, we must give them the ability to run, to step syllable by syllable into space, to give them feet. The Greeks had a strong and lively feeling for this in their dancing measures of dactyl, anapaest and so on. We can take simple lines that create, through their rhythm, the sensation of stepping through the words. This quality of stepping through needs to be retained even for the most mundane, arbitrary or broken dialogue, as we saw earlier in this book. The actor should seek to speak the line—however conventional—with this hidden dynamic of stepping through the syllables beneath the surface expression.

The necessity for this is only too evident if we consider how we speak nowadays. It could be compared to a poor violinist who rests his bow heavily on the strings and scrapes backwards and forwards, creating vibrations that are only a caricature of a musical tone. He would be blamed, most of all, for not releasing the note from the instrument.

It is the same with speech today. The tone does not escape from the speech box, so that the sound is grey and static. We have forgotten that our speech should move forwards and away from the speaker, towards the listener. If you mean what you say, and wish most sincerely for a listener to understand what you say, and finally, appreciate that the listener really listens to what you say, then one must move towards the idea that speaking is a human deed, just as real as running or moving things, or any other visible gesture.

If the actor speaks his lines as if they were stepping or dancing out before him, then what he says becomes important to the listener. If he breathes out the words, releasing them as though on the breath, he will come across as meaning what he says. If he does neither of these things, then the listener will feel the speaker does not mean what he is saying. In daily life, we often let out utterances without really thinking or meaning what we say, and our conversation consequently degenerates into mere chat. The actor who merely mimics the behaviour patterns of everyday life may get away with it in the sense that he is only doing what everyone does. But if he is to see acting as an art, he must maintain the artistic process, which is the lifeblood of his work, however outwardly 'natural' the speech may appear.

EXERCISE: STEPPING THE SYLLABLES

Dactylic
Flying away from us
Flowing away from us
Swimming away from us
Sailing away from us
Running away from us
Riding away from us

Iambic
I fly away
I flow away
I swim away
I sail away
I run away
I ride away

Trochaic
Flying faster
Flowing faster
Swimming faster
Sailing faster
Running faster
Riding faster

Anapest
Let us fly and be free
Let us flow and be free
Let us swim and be free
Let us sail and be free
Let us run and be free
Let us ride and be free

Try to carry the sound with the breath, as though the sound is dropped on to the breath stream and flows out into space.

The 'Substance' of Speech

Rudolf Steiner described speech in the theatre as having 'substance'. This I have found to be a most accurate description of what an actor can possess in his speaking. In England, our more mature actors and actresses have something of that quality in their traditional speaking. In the past, the manner in which actors formed their speech might have seemed quaint to our ears, but they had power and substance and, above all, they 'spoke' their lines, they did not 'say' them. Forgive me for harking back to the old days again, but increasingly performers are merely 'saying' their lines. The size of the theatre may cause them to shout, but forcing the volume of their voice is not enough to fulfil the demands of the theatre building.

There are four ingredients in producing the speaking voice: breath, tone, with which we are familiar; movement in space; and consonantal form which takes hold of the breath-system, i.e., articulation projected onto the moving breath, which is an invisible, ephemeral but extremely real, sculptural activity.

To speak your lines consciously, however contemporary in style the play may be, provides a firm platform for the expression of thoughts and feelings. If the 'substance' or the 'platform' is not there, the actor has no material from which to fashion expressive speaking and so he forces his voice, which we describe as cutting through space, not forming it.

What is the difference between just 'saying' a line and 'speaking' your lines? To 'speak' a line is to be conscious of each sound that makes up a word. This may seem an impossible demand but becomes easy and instinctive after a time, through habit and training. The conscious forming of words can be hidden behind whatever style of delivery, such as regional accents or quaint mannerisms, the play demands.

The breath must support the sound, which flows through the mouth and resonates in the air. We are familiar with resonators in the pharynx, mouth cavity, nose and sinus cavities to impress the tones on the air, but this is not what we are after. This vocal tone must be joined by movement in speaking. If the speaker/actor can impel vowels and consonants into the air instead of retaining them within the mouth, then they create travelling patterns in space where he can almost see the sounds as they perform invisible gymnastics before him.

Human speech is more expressive than gesture or mime. It reaches into the listener, and should play a much larger part in drama than it does today.

The breath-forms affect the listener more deeply than the vibration of the air on the ear-drum. The consonants reflect in us as we listen the formed realities of the world whereas the vowels pour out the feelings and reactions to these realities. There is an approximate ratio of three consonants to one vowel in most words. The consonants form a vessel which carries the vowel quality, which is gentler and expresses the soul of the human being. If we preserve expression and musicality in the moving sound, the substance of drama retains the ability to 'move' the audience. The actor must also feel that he affects the air and space in the whole theatre when he moves on the stage. The rest— character, plot, situation, interpretation—follow after.

Exclamation and Inner Gesture

Suppose we accept that human sound is the result of inner human gesture. Try thinking of all human sound as an *exclamation* resulting from the inner depths of the human being.

Then if we take the five vowel sounds as a field of study, each sound, each vowel, becomes, as it were, a jewel of human experience, a jewel crystallizing that inner world of human experience which, as yet, 'we know not of'.

The vowel 'ah' can indicate what inner gesture we are making when we speak it. We get a hint from the facial gesture made when 'ah' is pronounced. The mouth opens wide, so that the 'ah' sound seems to come out from the very depths of the speaker. So 'ah' can convey amazement or astonishment. Through this sound, the very psyche of a man can pour out.

An 'ee' sound, with the mouth not so open but somewhat stretched, and the teeth slightly bared, suggests a different gesture. Whereas the 'ah' sound can express a 'far off' mood, the distance of a 'star', the 'ee' can reflect our 'glee', the stretch of the 'sea', the feeling of being 'free', and so tends to suggest that we are asserting ourselves.

'O' has a surrounding quality, as in 'bowl' or 'fold'. The 'eh' quality as in 'send' or 'bend' has perhaps a holding-off quality. One class in England seems to colour the whole language with the 'eh' sound, as if they were 'fending off' the world.

The 'oo' or 'u', which by the shaping of the mouth seems to blow down a tube, contracts us, grips us, brings us something of sudden surprise, even of fear.

In the world of familiar sounds we utter, sometimes carelessly or mechanically, there lies a world of gesture that can be relived again in the speaking of them.

Becoming Familiar with the Sounds we Speak

I have referred to the gestures that lie in individual sounds. One can believe that all spoken sounds initially sprang from an exclamation of wonder or fear, and so forth. We can illustrate something of this experience in a simple exercise. We pretend to drop an egg; with amazement we gaze at the broken egg on the floor and exclaim 'Ah'. Another egg slips from our hand and the resulting mess on the floor arouses disgust. We cry 'Eh' (German 'ä' or 'ae' as in English 'sell'). Another one drops on the floor. We cease to care, and cry 'i' (ee), almost mixing in delight if not hysteria. Another drops, we cry 'Oh' in shock and dismay. Finally the last one falls, and we contemplate the whole mess with fear and anxiety, crying Oo ('u').

Thus, we have gone simply through the five vowel-sounds, discovering again the unity of human *im*pression and experience with sound *ex*pression. Now reversing the process, let the sounds speak to us, perhaps revealing their nature. One actor stands, and speaks sounds of his own choosing. The rest of the group listen, and move freely, reflecting the sounds they hear as movements.

For example, he may speak a particular kind of 's' sound, a hissing sound, rather than the 's' we say in the alphabet. Or else his 'k' may be said with the sharp palate sound as in 'kick', rather than 'kay'; and the 'f' sound as in 'puff' and so on, speaking both consonants and vowels. The listeners move, transforming the sound impression into a movement *ex*pression. In such a way we become familiar with the sounds we hear and speak.

In this exercise, a responsibility necessarily lies on the speaker—because, if he or she does not enjoy the discovery of the sounds as experienced during speaking them, then all is lost. It can be quite a shock when one realizes that the group are listening, hoping to gain something from one's delivery of the sounds. This responsibility helps towards awareness of the sounds and of the gestures that lie within them.

Next, the speaker can form a word, sound by sound, such as 'W-A-V-(e)', or 'H-A-T-(e)', or 'F-E-A-(r)', or 'T-R-E-E', pausing between each sound, so that the group comes to feel the form of each word.

The Inner Intonations: Some More Exercises

As a group we speak the five vowel sounds, letting each of them have its full expression before we sound the next. We then bring each of the five sounds into a short couplet to give us a sentence:

Ah   Far harder was the path that's past,
           But here at last, here lies the task.

Ae   To fail alone one cannot lay the blame,
           The failure tames the brain to start again.

Ee   To feel free, steals from eternity
           A fleeting glimpse of seen reality.

O   Fold the loam that binds the bone,
           Where seed be sown and shown new grown.

U(oo) Who flew from the tomb,
           Who flew from the hollow room.

Next we play out a scene that proceeds in turn through each of the five vowel sounds. It is a kind of *Oedipus* story. In amazement the people of Thebes gaze at themselves and see that all are struck with a mysterious plague, 'Ah'. Then, in the mood of 'ae', they pull themselves together and prepare to deal with the misery that has struck them. So, in the defiant mood of 'ee', they make their way towards the palace of Oedipus. He appears upon the steps and they express in 'o' their love for him and in the feeling of 'oo' prove it by assuming a mood of strength and readiness to serve.

He reveals that he is to blame for their misery. They are amazed and in turn set themselves against him, each pointing an accusing finger at him, although for a moment they have a feeling of passing sorrow for his fate, finally turning to face the future with fear, but also with resolution. With this exercise we have again felt our way through the five vowel sounds as moods of the soul. In this way we can be aware of their qualities as single sounds. At the same time, we can note their effect on expression in single words and finally as moods that colour whole speeches. The particular sound-mood chosen can be echoed in the choice of words, as illustrated here, but this is not always necessary.

First mime the action, with someone softly reading the text to guide us through the scene. Then we can perform the scene in our gibberish, colouring the progressive change of attitude as it develops, by using the appropriate vowel sounds.

Next we may mime the action, but gently sing the vowel sounds as a tone-key for each sequence. Having brought the movement and the underlying sound in harmony we can perform the scene in our 'gibberish', colouring the language with the vowel qualities, gestures and by the tone-keys. In this illustration the text echoes the vowel qualities which helps to guide us into each mood.

CHORUS:

Ah   Why has this disaster, this catastrophe come to us? Crops under harsh skies stand stark or are cast down, fear prowls through our towns, darkness lies in every heart, for all are blasted by the same plague.

Ae   Yet fate must not disable and crush us. Let us stand against it—save ourselves. Let us make our way to the palace gates where we may see the King.

Ee   Oedipus! King Oedipus! The city needs you. Be to us a priest and rid us of this evil. Give us freedom from this disease which has us in its grip.

O   Oh! Now the door opens. Behold the King—our hope

of overcoming the chaos around us, his robe a token of Olympian power.

U (oo)   We look to you O King . . . our duty is to you and to our country. Tell us truthfully the will of the gods revealed to you and it shall be done

[*The King confesses his guilt.*]

CHORUS:

Ah   It is hard to grasp! The past into the present casts deadly bane.

Ae   This sets him against us—us against him whom we said would save us, lead us.

Ee   But he himself is evil. Leave the city O Oedipus, no longer to be King.

O   Go! No one can know what sorrows shall follow you.

U(oo)   The rotten wood must be rooted out so that the future may bear good fruit.

The physical gestures in the movement and attitude of the chorus blend with the sound gestures, creating the progressive moods through the sequence, united with the content of the text. At this moment it is as though the chorus have become a 'body of expression'—the will appearing in the gesture, supporting the feelings of the chorus shown in their voice tones which are clarified by the content of the text in the intellect. This chorus body can finally extend their individual gesture into a group gesture. Thus at the beginning of the sequence, as a group, they are open and scattered. In the second part of the sequence, they travel across the stage, some moving in opposite directions to others, as they begin to unite. Now, they form themselves like a spear with a leader at the front as they call for Oedipus, then surround the King as he approaches. Finally they stand in two parallel lines from the back of the stage down to the front, as they speak of duty and resolution. Upon hearing that the blame lies with Oedipus, they again scatter and rebuild the group for the exit.

105

EXERCISE: VOWEL SOUNDS AS INNER EXCLAMATIONS

Try the following little mimes. Choose whatever outward gestures you think appropriate. The point is that secretly and invisibly you add the sound qualities. Remember, because we do not speak does not mean that we are *inwardly* silent.

He (or she) enters and, hearing voices in a room, listens at the door: AH. Suddenly the door opens: AE (he jumps back). He explains why he is there, telling some fantastic story: EE. He is not believed. He pleads for forgiveness: O. He is threatened with dismissal and is left standing alone, shocked: OO. (*Note*: A colleague can act the other role, otherwise just imagine it.)

She enters her flat, exhausted and relieved to be home: AH. She sees it has been entered and disturbed: EH. She sees a particular ornament has been broken: EE. She tries to mend it: O. And then she becomes aware that she is not alone: OO.

He sees a letter waiting for him: AH. He is uncertain what it may contain: EH. He opens it slowly. It is from someone he loves: EE. He reads it: O. The letter tells him that the friendship must end: OO. He is crushed.

The Consonants and the Four Elements

The consonants, we may find, are more descriptive of objects and events, whereas the vowels have more to do with inner expression. The consonants were related by Rudolf Steiner to the four elements:

Earth sounds	P B T D K G M N
Water sounds	L
Air sounds	R (rolled)
Fire sounds	F V W Th J Sh S Z Y H

By recalling that a word is created from a series of sound qualities (listed opposite) one may begin to picture the content of a word. A word may contain only consonants that are listed here as Earth sounds. Thus such words as DARK, DOOM, DEAD, when spoken, may noticeably contain a quality different from words containing 'Water' sounds—LULL, LILY, LOVELY. (NB: we are not so much concerned here with the relationship of sound and meaning, rather with feeling the *quality* of sound formation.)

The Air sound, 'R' rolled, gives us the experience of ROAR, AIR, and EERIE. The fire sounds give us SAFE, FISH and WAIF.

Or one word can combine two qualities. For instance, Water and Earth will provide us with the musical sound of LOAM, LIFT, LADLE. See how the liquid quality of the 'L' sound is either gently or abruptly given a firm shape by the following Earth sound and then, in the example of LADLE, is released again into the Watery form, or sharply held by the 'T' in LIFT. We can melt the Earthly sound into a Watery element as with POOL, BOWL, MOLE. Such imaginations when speaking words also provide us with the experience of moving through a word rather than feeling it as a series of sounds pressed together. Thus with MOLE we can move from the 'M' to the 'O' to the 'L', and so live through the experience of the total word. Let us take 'Air' to 'Fire' sounds, RUSH, ROUSE, RIFE, 'Earth' to 'Fire' DAZE, BUSH, DASH.

Moving Through a Word

Take a word and speak it, sound by sound. Repeat each sound of the word individually, so that others listening can dance to the individual sounds though unable to recognize the complete word. Here is an example: S-s-s-s-s-s- repeated; then, T-t-t-t-t-t- repeated in all ways, slowly, quickly, lightly and so forth; then, E-e-e-e-e-e-e-, in high or low tones, playing with the sound as an individual exercise. The actors and actresses should dance, gesturing and moving to these sounds in their individual way. Finally comes the sound L-l-l-l-l-l-l-. The speaker then says the complete word, *steal*.

We can choose any word and bring it by way of mime into a dance pattern. Such words as *bind, fly, loose, tight, dead, life, fear, brave*. It can be interesting to discover words that, out of movement, describe themselves—*free, catch, hate, love*, and so on. The sounds often describe the meaning of a word, but it is enough that we begin to visualize the gesture within words and, as Steiner suggests, 'let actors and actresses feel that they are "swimming" in the sounds' when they dance to the sounds and the speaker feels that he is 'tasting' the sounds.

Steiner's expression 'tasting' is not as strange as it may seem. A speech written with a feeling for sound complements the sense of the lines with meaning in the sound. W.B. Yeats said, when asked how he created a poem, 'I made it out of a mouthful of air.'

From the few words listed above, we can create brief mimes, inwardly intoning the sounds. Take the word, *Steal* again. The S-s-s-s-s brings us onto the stage; perhaps we shape our mouth as though saying S-s-s, but all in silence of course. Feel this sound in the eyes as well, and the sharpness of the 'T' sound. 'T' is followed by the penetrating of E-e-e-e-e which leads us to *see* what we steal, the final L-l-l-l-l gathering the object stolen. We know the meaning of the word but, even so, we can bring the word to life through its sound. An increasing awareness for the sound in words would counteract a prevalent indifference to the musicality of speech.

Rudolf Steiner, in his book *Eurythmy as Visible Speech*, gave a list of sounds together with a brief description of the movement and quality of them.

ah	Wonder. Amazement
b	To wrap round; to envelop
c (ts)	The quality of lightness
d	To indicate; to ray outwards
e	To be affected by something and to withstand it
t	A significant streaming from above downwards
ee	Assertion of self

l	The overcoming of matter by form
m	To be in agreement
u	The becoming chilled and stiffened
sch	The blowing past of something
r	Rolling, revolving
a	Wonder
ei	The quality of clinging

Also, in his *Speech and Drama* course, Steiner gave a few illustrations of sound expressions.

Fear	oo		
Pity	ei	Compassion	
Awe	ah	Wonder	
Curiosity	ee		
Assertion	ee		
Pointing	d, t	Schoolmaster	
Embrace the world	ee, o	Self-admiration	
Anger	ee, ae	Tension-release	
Sorrow/terror	ae	(as in 'sale')	
Acute concern	All sounds but through compressed lips		
Whole attention	ah.ah.ah . . .		
Surprise	ee.ee.ee . . .		
Terror	oo		
Contempt	n.n.n . . .		
Dejection	v-ae		
Rapture	h		
Careful reflection	ah-o ah-o		

EXERCISE: KEY SIGNATURES FOR THE ACTOR

Circle scene

The group stands in a circle. Each performer takes a line of the dialogue in turn, first preparing by 'tuning in' with the sound given at the margin.

At first, the tuning in may be audible, and perhaps repeated two or three times before speaking the line.

Later on, speak the line, and only inwardly intone the sound gesture. The speech is directed to an unfortunate prisoner in the centre of the circle.

Sound gesture into expression of sentence. Exclamation

Ah	Now I begin to understand.
Ae	I must say you have a nerve.
O	My dear fellow, you are putting on a bold face.
Ee	I can see that he is upset.
U	You are all so cruel, leave him/her alone.
Ee	Yes, leave him in peace.
O	For pity's sake, be finished now.
Ah	So I am to suffer treason within our circle.
U	No, I did not say that.
O	Only have pity.
Ee	Let him go free!
Ae	And escape? You must be mad! Take no notice of these weaklings.
Ee	What does *he/she* have to say?
N	Nothing, he will say nothing!
D	He dare not.
F	Fear prevents him.
K	So cruelty will kill him!
M	His silence moves me to compassion.
Ee	It is the silence of innocence.
G	Of guilt. ▶

110

F	Of fear.
D	Of despair.
R	Release him, let him go free.
G	And forget him.
T	That's it, exile him and forget him.
D	It shall be done.

Muttered Thoughts

The following exercises take us beyond movement and sound expressions into dialogue.

First, we describe a situation. Someone, say, has lost something and is searching for it. As the actor mimes his search he begins to 'mutter', as one can quite easily do in such a situation, 'muttering', 'sighing', 'exclaiming', and so forth. From such primitive beginnings it is possible for quite a reasonable speech to occur. However, the main object of the exercise is to bring our expression into phrases and sentences. The burgled flat story (p. 106) that we have already used in mime and in inner sounding can finally be handled with 'muttered' dialogue.

Our muttered thoughts are now put down as text—that is how the following little speeches originated. They originally were five short dialogues, but the performers can run them together for the purpose of an exercise.

In speaking them, use not only the vowels but also the consonants to 'colour' the content of the lines.

STORM BLOWING

Character 1

Ah   Look there, afar, see, approaching,
Like a mist, a low lying cloud,
That swiftly travels over the earth.
Ah! How it comes to overwhelm.
What magic spell is woven here,
That brings this midnight to the stars?

111

Character 2

B   Bind and bend yourself about,
        Protect with cloak our lonely forms,
        And again, let not the darkness
        Penetrate the folds, hold, hold your cloak,
        Let not the black wind pluck the garments
                            from our backs.

Character 1

M   Move through this mist with a certain care,
        With measured tread and firm resolve,
        Undaunted by this mystery—the unknown—
                   that which may or may not be.
        Come! Mould your thoughts to calmer forms.

Character 2

Eh   Stay! Step not a pace further,
        Let fear hold us firm, let strength of our suspicions,
        The doubts we share, act as a shield,
        A strong defence, against that which awaits us there.

Characters 1 and 2 take 'Ee' and 'D' respectively—

D   As this dense and dark thing draws near, I stand secure,
        Bound to this solid earth. This gives me strength to
                    endure what should daunt me.

Ee   But we must penetrate the mist and seek to discover its
                                  meaning.

D   I have forebodings, draw back and stand firm.

Ee   See! I do not fear, but erect prepare to meet whate'er the
                                  mist reveals.

D   There and there, those objects there!

Ee   Now I see them—Oh how my keen desire bids me to
                                perform deeds.

Characters 1 and 2 take O and N respectively—

O   Oh let me fold you in my cloak, hold you near, protect you.
Oh do not turn away!

N   No! Now is the moment when I must stand alone.

O   Alone! Who is alone? It is I that am alone.

N   Nearer and nearer comes the storm.

O   O my son, return to your loved ones, your home.
Do not go, do not go.

N   Never, into this night I step, in I step, in I step.

O   Foul darkness overwhelms him.

Characters 1 and 2 take R and U respectively—

R   Terror grips my heart; I cannot help but tremble as the storm approaches.

U   Be resolute! This cruel wind shall not move us.

R   Oh, I am freezing, let us return.

U   No, we must go on through it.

R   Oh, this raging wind is carrying me away.

U   Stoop low and with your shoulder push.

Point of Speech Exercises

The purpose of introducing such a foundation as we have been describing for speech is to give the actor the opportunity to rise up from the ashes of naturalism.

Having lost a truly natural sense for speaking, and for sounds, for words, for listening, he has had to compensate for his loss with an unnatural tension in speech and in expression.

This very *un*-naturalness is increasingly considered as if it were normal behaviour. Now the actor has to hold the mirror up to *nature*—but his work is being threatened when he has to ape these 'normal' manners and conventions which for the most part are really quite *ab*normal.

I suspect that this situation at the same time causes the actor to rely on naturalism, because he is becoming increasingly unable to move beyond it, so that acting is reduced to behaviour and speaking is diminished to mere saying.

CHAPTER 10
Epic, Dramatic and Lyric Moods

Drama was not a pastime that sprang up out of nowhere as a game of charades that developed into art. It had its place in the ancient Mystery schools from whence it was released into the world, but in a changed form. We know the story of the actor Thespis who stepped out of the chorus and depicted a character to speak opposite the chorus, from which came duologue. Other characters stepped out of the chorus until a play was born with a chorus commenting on the action. This is how historians describe the appearance of drama.

We must add to this description, however, the fact that drama developed three distinct styles. The first style was that of the epic speaker, the reciter or story-teller. Then there was what was called the lyric or declaiming style; the performer spoke from personal feelings of longing and desire, or private woes or triumphs. This was quite opposite to the epic style and also delivered in a way quite different from that of the speaker of epic. Between the epic and lyric styles was the dramatic style, where at least two people took part, as in a conversation.

So we had the epic reciter, the dramatic conversation, and the declaiming lyric speaker. Each performer or performers possessed a trained style of speaking. These were based on three qualities which were believed to be part of the human soul. The epic style used our ability for creative thinking, imagination and memory. The dramatic style showed the human ability to converse, sharing thoughts and ideas, and creating social activity. At the beginning, the height of human activity was thought to be the art of conversing; only later was it thought of as conflict. The lyric was a personal outpouring from the human being—a song of despair, or of joy or hope.

115

It is possible to understand that Homer, the epic speaker, lost nothing of his art through being blind. Not only did the epic speaker dream his fantasy, recalling ancient tales, but he placed his voice more to the back of the mouth, the soft palate. The position was believed to release the *will* of the speaker which played an important part in the forming of thoughts and images in his speaking style. This style would in turn stimulate the will of the listeners, and so they too could create inner pictures.

The lyric speaker, the singer, pouring out his heart to the listener, was not concerned with the past or with pictures but with his present state of mind and very much with his future. He sang out with a longing for the future, seeing his destiny as a path guiding him towards his fate. This impulse to look forward was also present in his speaking which was set forwards on the lips, where it was believed the waves of feeling life poured out to the listener. The open mouth became the expression of feeling and passion. The ancient Egyptian statues stand as though dreaming with the mouth closed and the eyes seeing into another world. The Greek statues and paintings show the mouth open as though a new experience in this world had arrived in their civilization— lyrical speaking flowing with feeling out of the mouth as a song of the individual soul.

Standing between the epic and lyric speakers are two persons. They are actors; they speak to each other, the spoken thoughts of one stimulating thought in another. Drama lived in the space between them. So the actor's speech is placed in the centre of the mouth where the mobile tongue is working with the hard palate and teeth.

We have the epic speaker standing up-stage, invoking the area behind him. He is like the spear thrower before he throws. He calls in his thoughts from the periphery.

Drama exists centre-stage where the action is in the present; it is happening now, wide awake and brilliant with thoughts.

The lyric speaker is down-stage, nearest to the listeners, speaking to them personally, the spear in full flight. These three qualities are as alive in us in the present day as they were in ancient times. Style means nothing if it has no basis in reality. Style is a truth in life clarified from observation and shaped by the artist.

116

Today, when a person tries to remember some event, you can see them disappear into themselves and search around in the memory or, filled with concern or passion for their situation, they burst out in exasperation or anxiety when telling you their state of mind. They may pace the floor, giving full reign to their feelings and opinions, not wishing you to answer them or correct them, or suggest another point of view—they are in full, lyrical mood. The dramatic mood arises from the curious intensity that comes about when two people exchange views in a discussion. It is the choice of words and the manner in which they are spoken that effects the other person. No dreaming, as in epic style, no lyrical outbursts, but an alert awareness of the way a discussion or conversation is going leads us towards drama.

In theatre, the *drama* appears from the activity of two or more characters on the stage. In the soliloquy or *lyrical* poetry, the soul appears alone, as though breathing out. In epic, the creativity of the story-teller appears as ideas and pictures from another world. When one plays scenes it is possible to observe these three qualities shifting in the behaviour of a character. The difference may not be obvious to the spectator though he or she will inwardly sense the rightness of the lines spoken and their placement in a speech, whether it be lyrical, epic or dramatic.

First we will perform a strong exercise to be carried out with intensity. Let it be melodramatic or exaggerated, as they say, for it is only when we are fully committed to it that something may be experienced.

Start up-stage as though sensing a force behind you, then meet a colleague in the centre of the stage and, finally, rush forward to pour out your heart down-stage.

Epic: up-stage
    Listening, listening, I hear whispering,
    Distant beckoning, reaching, pleading, picturing
    Glistening, echoing, beckoning, conjuring,
    Misting, forming, storming, stronger making,
    Shapes partaking, stories calling, forming, forming.

Dramatic: centre-stage
    Such tales I have to tell you, such mysteries. Will you believe

117

me? I see you smile. A clown, you say. A fool. A dreamer. A tool of fantasy! But I tell you, my friend, when I have finished, you will agree, you will accept and not reject, the tales I tell.

Lyric: down-stage
Oh, if only I could release the magic of those moments. Oh, such dreams, such memories. How can I ever express in tame words the conjured magic. Oh, what purpose can there be in witnessing magic worlds if my words cannot pass on those moments? O Muse! I invoke you. Speak through me! Let me show the mystery that I know.

I have put together a conventional scene that contains the qualities—epic, dramatic, lyric—we have just discussed though not in such an obvious form; a lyrical quality may only appear for a moment in a couple of words or a character may briefly reflect in the epic mood. If you feel a shift in space as you speak lines that appears to belong to one of the three quality areas we have spoken about, you are developing an inner sense of movement.

RECALL

FATHER (*an elderly invalid*). I can recall, not so very long ago, that we quarrelled on some matter. What it was I can only faintly remember, something concerning money. A debt? A loan? Something concerning money, I know. Some loss or some finding? Some injustice? What was it, that caused us such pain and anguish? Can you remember, my boy?

SON. No, Father. It must have been some time ago.

FATHER. But can you remember?

SON. No, I say. It's all forgotten.

FATHER. What is forgotten?

SON. What are you trying to remember? Give me patience!

FATHER. What?

SON. Nothing, Father.

FATHER. Wait! I think I have it. It was to do with my will.

SON. Oh no! Light up your pipe, Father, enjoy the evening.

FATHER. I begin to recall it now. I had got out my will to add a codicil to it.

SON. God! I think he will drive me mad.

FATHER. What?

SON. I said, I think you will drive me mad.

FATHER. Why?

SON. You are talking about a time when you dreamt up the idea that I was a bad lot and that my brother should have all your money and I none.

FATHER. So what did I do?

SON. Changed your will.

FATHER. So your brother has all?

SON. Yes . . . but unfortunately Harry is now dead.

FATHER. Oh my God! Harry, dear Harry. I remember him as a lad. So neat, always so clean. So bright, like a new penny . . . and such a naughty grin and yet so wise. He always seemed to me so wise. He would frighten me when, with his grave eyes, he would gaze at me unsmiling suddenly. He died of pneumonia, did he not?

SON. Yes, Father.

FATHER. You did not like him, did you my son?

SON. No! He was a wiseacre and a smart little cub. Cheeking me, because I was older and not letting me be older and wiser than him . . . and he would look at me with those old eyes of his . . . 'Wise Eyes' I would call him, and then regret having said it because it made him sound wiser than me. What a pest he was! So smart, so clever, so clean. Now, he's dead and I'm alive.

FATHER. In my heart, he is not dead. His every movement haunts my memory. The sound of his voice—he would whisper sometimes and then laugh and run away when I asked him what he had said.

SON. A few moments ago you didn't remember he was dead.

FATHER. It is true. I still can't believe it. To me, he is still alive.

SON. Well, he is dead, so let's say no more about it.

FATHER. Now I remember what you did to make me so angry!

SON. So you remember. So *I* remember . . . but now let's forget it. It's some time ago and there are better ways of spending the evening than talking about old memories.

FATHER. Yes . . . I remember. You tried to persuade the authorities that I was mad and not responsible for the setting down of my will.

SON. Well, you were mad. But now I think I will go mad myself—just stop talking.

FATHER. If the money did not go to Harry, where did it go?

SON. Just stop it! It's more than I can bear! This old man has been the bane of my life! That's the truth! The bane of my life!

FATHER. What are you saying?

SON. That you have been the bane of my life. A pest! A wiseacre!

FATHER. Like Harry!

SON. God give me peace and rest from this old man of the sea!

FATHER. Where did the money go?

SON. I have it.

FATHER. How?

SON. Why ask? Why ask? God, why doesn't he stop? Why does he go on? Leave it, Father. Just leave it!

FATHER. What did you do with the money?

SON. It didn't work out as I planned. I planned to get it by convincing the authorities you were not sane.

FATHER. And you failed!

SON. No, I succeeded. God help me! I succeeded! The only thing I have ever succeeded at!

FATHER. You succeeded. How?

SON. Because you are here.

FATHER. Here? This is my home.

SON. It is not your home.

FATHER. No! Now I remember. We had a veranda. The veranda. The lawn. The staircase in the centre of the house. The black iron stove. The blinds, the curtains, the sewing machine in the corner. . . Where is it all?

SON. Gone!

FATHER. Gone?

SON. This is *a* home. I told you—I succeeded!

FATHER. My memory must have gone but not my mind.

SON. True, but now it's too late.

FATHER. And you have the money . . . and Harry is dead. Oh, Harry, I wanted so much to help you. You deserved help. I could have helped you. I could have set you up. Now you are gone and the money is gone.

SON. Yes, Father. It's being used to keep you here. It's supporting you. I didn't get it, I only got the joke. You see the joke? The money is supporting you in the trap I laid.

CHAPTER 11
Exercises for Lyric, Epic and Dramatic Speaking

By Barbara Bridgmont

To begin with, here are some exercises to awaken our sense for consonant placement. You will remember the picture of the mouth as having a back area (up-stage), a middle area (centre-stage) and a forward area (down-stage). These three areas in the mouth express different qualities in human behaviour regardless of the meaning of the words spoken. We must develop a sense of sound in speaking before it expresses feelings or thoughts. The sounds tell you, as you speak, about themselves. Here are a few simple exercises which, although helpful as technical training for speaking, have not been devised for that purpose alone. First we seek to develop a feeling for the position in the mouth of the consonants that dance through the line.

The consonants in the first 'gymnastic' (**1**), as we might call these lines of sound, are mainly in a forward (lyrical) placement in the mouth, 'downstage'. In (**2**) we have the middle and in (**3**) the back (epic) placement.

Speak these sentences while standing on the corresponding area of the stage.

1   Warm waves move over from washed pebbles.

      Blow those bright rainbow bubbles,
      Impossible to pursue.

      Why, oh why, will you push for impossibly improbable promises?

2 **A** Dare to trudge down town to tantalizing treats.
  B Too dangerous.
  A No one need know.
  B Not my line.

  A I say that this riddle should test the intelligence that rules by the light of reason. Let all stand this trial.
  B No! Don't say that! It is not right to test the intellect alone. Each heart also has its statement.

3 He cleaved then carved the crystalline rock,
   Creating greatest glory.

   Gagged by gargantuan hags in ghastly caves, they kicked, hacked, struggled with the cackling crew.

   So came the Turk, his galleons glistering gold,
   His crescent flags crimson 'gainst darkening clouds.
   Then cracked heaven's thunder and black squalls attacked
   The groaning ships. Great cataracts across
   The decks crashed; helms splintered, chaos broke out.

   _____

Next some sense nonsense, but sound 'sound sense'.

Cook a cake.	*or*	He cooks cakes
Hug a hag		He hugs hags
Kick a hog		He kicks hogs
Cork a keg		He corks kegs
Hook a key		A car-key hook has he

All the consonants on the left are at the back; those on the right are the same, but coming to the middle for the S sounds.

   _____

TWENTY DIMPLED TEMPLE DANCERS
Swings between middle and front.
TW NT D MPL D T MPL D NC   S

123

LACK A TINGLING DRINK TO TAKE
Swings between middle and back.
L   K   T NGL NG DR NK T   T   K

NOBLE NEIGHBOURS NAMED IN NAPLES
Swings between middle and front.
N BL N   B   S N M D N N PL S

NECK AND NECK ON KNOCK-KNEED NAGS
Swings between middle and back.
N   K   ND N   K   N   N   K   N   D N GS

If one moves physically on the stage, mirroring the placement of the consonant sounds, the speech will gain much in liveliness and clarity; also the consciousness of the speaker will begin to take hold of the sounds.

It is essential that we do not think that the placement is where the sound 'sounds'. It is where it originates, but then it must be breathed forward so that it is carried on the breath in front of the speaker. That is why we sometimes talk about seeing the sounds and even sensing where they are in space. For training, we might make a picture of speaking words which fly forwards, like a painter throwing paint from his brush. The paint strikes his canvas well in front of him and he can consider the pattern that his painted word has made.

Grab and grip	(From the back to the front of the mouth, i.e. from the soft palate to the lips. Each word)
Brick and block	(From the front to the back of the mouth. Each word)
Tit for tat	(From the middle of the mouth. Tongue and teeth)
That's that	(From the middle of the mouth. Tongue and teeth)

Again—

Crumbs and cream	(From the back to the front of the mouth)

124

Make or break	(From the front to the back of the mouth)
To eat or not	(From the middle of the mouth)
Don't do it	(From the middle of the mouth)

So far so good.

Note—now that we have experimented with the consonant sounds for ourselves, we may tabulate them for the sake of clarity, but please become familiar with them by speaking the exercises.

K
L
S
F
M

The placement of each consonant in the above list takes the sound step by step from the back of the mouth to the front. Pace down the room, with each step a sound, until you have stepped the five consonants. Make one silent step, and then again, feeling that your speech, as well as yourself, is moving forward.

Gradually increase the pace of stepping and the flow of speaking these consonants. In this way, we travel the whole distance within the mouth. Feel the sounds flow through the mouth from back to front.

Here we have a sample, as it were, of the various placements. Now, let us add the other sounds that exist in the five areas with their placement in the mouth.

Organs of Articulation	**Sounds**	**Example**
Soft palate and back of tongue	K	Kick
	G	Gig
	NG	Singing
	Y	Your yacht
Tip of tongue brushes against hard palate	R (brushed)	
Tip of tongue vibrates against hard palate	R (rolled)	Roaring river

125

Tip of tongue and front of hard palate (where the teeth join the hard palate)	L	Lily
	N	Nanny
	T	Taught
	D	Deed
Tip of tongue against front teeth	TH	Thick and thin (unvoiced)
	TH	Whither and thither (voiced)
Tongue, hard palate, lips are all used to guide the breath through the teeth and form the outgoing sound	S	Sister
	Z	Buzzes
	SH	She should
	ZH	Measure
Top teeth and bottom lip	F	Fife
	V	Revive
Both Lips	P	Poppy
	B	Bobbing
	M	Memo
	W	Well-wisher

Vowel Placement

Let us return to our stage and relate our position upon it to the placement of the vowels.

Stand at the back of the stage, open the whole vocal instrument fully and breath out the sound AH.

Move to the front of the stage, direct all the activity forward through the narrowly rounded lips and breathe out the sound OO.

Now we stand in the middle of the stage and speak EE.

AH — OO — EE   AH — OO — EE

Now let them flow in sequence from back to front (**1**):

(1) AH	**(2)** Ah	as in 'bard'
	Ay	as in 'paved'

126

EE		Ee	as in 'deed'
		Oh	as in 'gold'
OO		Oo	as in 'fooled'

Now slide 'ay' and 'oh' into place and we move through the 'mouth-stage':

AH — AY — EE — OH — OO (2).

Exercise: DIVE into the movement with these vowel sounds and RUN on into the silence.

Out of the movement in silence comes the movement and form in speech; then the movement and form of speech is released into the silence.

Where does the energy come from? Just from the speaker? Perhaps not.

The speaker calls in forces from the periphery. He is master of his physical vocal equipment. These two elements he uses as a sculptor uses medium and tools, to create a moving, invisible sculpture of breath and tone; they are then released into the space as life-bearing gifts to the listeners.

Exercise: Move silently
Stand for monophthong: AH.
Move through diphthong: AY.
Stand for monophthong: EE.
Move through diphthong: OH.
Stand for monophthong: OO.
Move on into silence.

Syllable Step

Exercise: PATH WAYS WE SHOW YOU
The same vowels as above—but this time take each vowel and move it by the energy of the consonant which precedes it towards the next syllable and so on into the silence. Physically step the syllable at the same time. Repeat until the physical movement can stop, leaving the speech to move in space.

'Sound Taste'—Epic—Dramatic—Lyric

Speak the following two sentences, noticing where the consonant sounds are placed.

a) I do not think it right to treat him so.
b) I would not be willing to proceed in this way.

Is it possible to sense out of the 'sound taste' alone a difference in quality between (**a**) and (**b**)?

Speak (**a**) in a strong, horizontal stream, throwing the middle consonants (d, n, t, r, s) like darts towards your partner. Sense the direction and control of idea which these hard-palate sounds give you.

Now try (**b**). In this sentence the lips seem to soften the direction of the breath-stream, with the repeated 'w' sound producing a more wave-like flow.

These laborious descriptions of speech sensations quickly become a matter of instinct for the speaker but require these few words of explanation.

Now let us speak a poem which bubbles with humour.

WHY SO PALE AND WAN?

Why so pale and wan, fond lover?
  Prithee, why so pale?
Will, when looking well can't move her,
  Looking ill prevail?
  Prithee, why so pale?

Why so dull and mute, young sinner?
  Prithee, why so mute?
Will, when speaking well can't win her,
  Saying nothing do't?
  Prithee, why so mute?

Quit, quit for shame! This will not move;
    This cannot take her.

If of herself she will not love,
    Nothing can make her.
    The devil take her!

The first two verses fall forward from the lips—the speaker mocking his friend's state of feeling (LYRIC). Then comes the advice and an abrupt change of placement with a more direct dynamic: 'Quit, quit for shame!' and so on (DRAMATIC).

Now we will speak the first verse of Yeats's poem, 'The White Birds'.

I would that we were, my beloved, white birds on the foam of
    the sea!
We tire of the flame of the meteor, before it can fade and flee;
And the flame of the blue star of twilight, hung low on the rim
    of the sky,
Has awaked in our hearts, my beloved, a sadness that may not
    die.

The rhythm and the strong forward placement gives the impression of the soul flowing out in waves of longing (LYRIC).

And now some lines from *Don Juan II*, by Lord Byron:

It was a wild and breaker-beaten coast,
    With cliffs above, and a broad sandy shore,
Guarded by shoals and rocks as by a host,
    With here and there a creek, whose aspect wore
A better welcome to the tempest-tost;
    And rarely ceased the haughty billow's roar,
Save on the dead long summer days, which make
The outstretch'd ocean glitter like a lake . . .

In the extract from *Don Juan II*, we notice how many of the strong soft-palate sounds have been used—excellent for the epic style.

The poets have done their part. Now, comes the speaker. It is not enough for him to 'feel' the lyric quality or to 'mean' his lines of dramatic dialogue.

To speak in a lyrical style means to speak in a style adapted for the expression of personal feelings. This does not mean the personal feelings of the verse speaker or actor. The poet has experienced the feelings and he has chosen to write them down.

How do we, the performers, restore to the poem that inspired energy, which must become lost in the writing down. Every actor has met several, if not many, methods for dealing with this problem. One method may be to return to the imagination of calling in the activity from the periphery (it makes a refreshing change from calling upon oneself).

Imagine a waterfall eternally falling and flowing away. Imagine the drops of spray, with the sun making rainbow colours. The poet has turned feelings into words. The speaker turns words into feelings by releasing the syllables like drops of water into the waterfall. The sounds of the words contribute immeasurably to the transference of feelings to the listener. He knows the life and purity of his sounds. He also knows how to control the direction of his outgoing breath. The right technique calls forth the right feeling.

Take the case of dialogue—conversation, argument. Here again the matter passed on is 'second-hand'. It is a strange truth, that the better a phrase is prepared beforehand the more spontaneous it sounds. Breathe in the line—go to the back space as the spear thrower, and release it horizontally.

The Epic Style

One of the oldest forms of the art of speech is epic (narrative, story-telling). Here, the pictures and actions in the story are what are important, what we want to *see*. The best story-teller is one who can 'disappear', leaving his story in his place—not at all easy. He, above all, must become a sculptor of the breath; his tools are the sounds (chiefly the consonants), his colours are the tones.

He stands firmly on the ground and speaks with the forces from his limbs. But these forces must dive into the breath-stream and step out into space, with the energy called from the periphery.

Against crusty crevised rocks
The horseman could not canter

130

Use the back sounds, K and G, to knead the syllables into form (almost like hands kneading dough), and then release them forward.

The Dactylic Hexameter

The oldest known metrical form into which epic verse was cast is the dactylic hexameter. As the name implies, it consists basically of six dactylic feet.

Let us bear in mind five things—

1) The structure of ancient Greek verse was based on *quantity*, i.e. length of syllable, one long syllable being equal to two short ones.
2) The spondee (— —) therefore could be substituted for the dactyl (— v v). This meant there was enormous elasticity in the line—the metre was rhythmically buoyant, spacious.
3) The last part of each line was never a full dactyl (— v v). Either it became a spondee (— —) or the last short of the dactyl was replaced by a pause (— v ˆ). This gives added flow to the ends of lines.
4) The in-breathing was regulated, not random, there being two spaces for the breath to each line. Each in-breath occupied the duration of one dactyl. Thus you had in each line eight spaces: two for inhaling and six spoken dactyls (or spondees). The pause for breath within the line is called the ceasura. This was not dead centre of the line.

Not as:

— v v / — v v / — v v / / — v v / — v v / — v v

But, as illustrated with a) b) and c), it had a movable position. The following are the most usual variants (I have not included substitution of spondees).

a)
— v v / — v v / — / / v v / — v v / — v v / — v / ˆ

b)
— v v / — v v / — v / / v / — v v / — v v / — — /

131

c)

— v v / — v v / — v v — / / v v / — v v / — — /

5) On pp.79–80, the relation of pulse beat to breath is dealt with. Thus we have a framework built on the same principles as the rhythmic system of the human being.

We have seen that the activity from the periphery plays into the breath-stream, and that in epic the forces of form take hold of that breath-stream in the sculptured consonants. We see how this metrical form creates a pulse which carries the narrative forward, providing *breathing spaces* for inspiration.

When you carry out the next exercise, sense the interplay between the two activities:

INSPIRATION → SPEECH → INSPIRATION → SPEECH

Become aware of the periphery as the breath streams into you—

IN   BREATHING

IN   SPIRATION

Become aware of the picture which you are about to describe and try to 'hear before' (Marie Steiner's expression) how the words should be delivered.

Then, in the out-streaming breath, shape the picture by your creative activity with and through the sounds of speech.

Exercise

Choose a long sound and a short sound, for example 'Dah' and 'Ti'. Speak these sounds, the long and the short on the metrical pattern, letting the breath become rhythmical sound and the activity of speech flow on into the silences. No content—only sound.

132

```
— v v  — v v  —  / /  v v  — v v  — v v  — —
— v v  — —   —  / /  v v  — v v  — v v  — v^
— —   — v v  —  v  / / v  — —   — —   — —
— v v  — v v  —  v  / / v  — v v  — v v  — v^
— —   — v v  —  v  v —/ / v v  — v v  — v^
— v v  — —   —  v  v —/ / v v  — v v  — —
```

The above are just some of the possible variations. It can be very amusing to find that in the break after a practise period with hexameters quite an effort is needed not to continue in this rhythm in everyday conversation!

The following is from Homer's *Odyssey*, Book V, translated into dactylic hexameters by H.B. Cotterill.

E'en as he spake from aloft/ /came crashing a billow enormous

Bursting terrific upon him/ / and whirling the quivering raft round.

Far from the raft he was swept by the wave,/ / and the rudder in falling

Loosed from the grip of his hand,/ / while clean in the middle the mast snapt,

Smit by the terrible blast/ / of the winds which met in a cyclone.

Far off on the waves/ / down clattered the sail with the yardarm.

Long did it keep him below/ /in the depths of the water, unable

Swiftly to rise, held back/ / by the rush of the mountainous rollers,

Weighed down too by his garment, / / the gift of the goddess Calypso.

Note: Owing to the accentual nature of English verse the translator of Greek hexameters needs to find, where possible, syllables which are both accented and *long*, to preserve the sound structure of the original.

My purpose in presenting these exercises is not primarily to try to create speakers among the readers. I simply wish to show that exercises, training, practice, theory and style come from an understanding of the human being and should not be a network of arbitrary instructions restricting the artistic activity of men and women. It should be a method of speaking and moving that is the essence of human endeavour remoulded into a training programme. Education of this kind does not impose laws and corrections but clarifies our activity and gives it style. This style should lie at the very foundation of dramatic performances.

CHAPTER 12
Deductive Drama

In this final chapter I am setting out two scenes, one for two men, the other for two women. They are simple scenes, written in an ordinary conversational style. I have coined a phrase to describe this kind of scene—'deductive drama'. The behaviour of the characters is familiar; they act and react within a conventional pattern, and we can understand the line of thought and direction of the emotions. From the characters' attitudes we can deduce how they feel and why they think as they do. We, the spectators, then bring something to the scenes, either from our own experiences in life or associations of ideas, and so we arrive at a certain attitude towards the action as we add our personal feelings. Take, for example, the scene with a mother arguing with her son's girl-friend (p.141). How you react to this scene may well depend upon whether you have experienced such arguments yourself. If you have not, then you may well wonder what the scene is really about. If you have, and you think the author has got it right, you may feel you have gained something from watching this scene because your memory has stirred you into recognizing familiar attitudes. When we watch a play, we could be surprised at the pleasure we gain from it simply because it is familiar to us. We are in a world we can manage. If the play is a farce and characters are hurrying in and out of embarrassing situations, we may not have experienced these situations but, because we are familiar with the surroundings, the bizarre happenings amuse us. We can watch a Chekhov play and be surprised at how much we understand because the characters' feelings are like our own.

A major criterion of enjoyment when watching a play today usually is that we can relate to it. The more one relives something of oneself in a play the more one approves of it. Now if we apply the same criterion to music, we could have a picture of a satisfied bourgeois audience. A picture gallery that catered for the familiar would have the same atmosphere. I believe that what is understood and recognized in other arts is not of the best, but in the theatre the success of naturalism relies entirely on this audience attitude. In fact, one suspects that the aim of many productions is to present to the audience the familiar and mundane, no matter what the subject or original style of the play may be. The actor and producer pander to the deductive drama, which does not force the audience to go far beyond their own behaviour or experience.

Whatever we do, we must bring the audience with us on a journey which either stretches the imagination or depicts human endeavour, in success or failure, as being inspired by inner convictions beyond the pragmatism of the familiar. How can this be attempted? Of course we look to playwrights and they can urge themselves to cross frontiers of thought and behaviour which may come as a surprisingly fresh outlook on the world. Has the actor anything to give in this direction?

Perhaps he must take more seriously the power of the invisible gesture in speech and movement. I will use the following two scenes to illustrate how we can develop along the lines I have mentioned.

THE CONSCIENTIOUS OBJECTOR

DAVID. Clifford! How good it is to see you again. Do come in. Don't stand outside.

[*Enter Clifford, limping with a stick*]

DAVID. Hurt your leg?

CLIFFORD. Yes, David, old lad. I hurt my leg. In fact it hurt so badly they had to take it off.

DAVID. Oh God, I'm sorry. Here, take this chair.

CLIFFORD. You don't have to do that. The rest of me is still capable. [*He sits*] So this is the little cottage you've told me so much about in your letters.

136

DAVID. Yes. [*Silence*] It's simple and primitive.

CLIFFORD. And safe, David, safe. While we fight a bloody war you—you sit here safe.

DAVID. [*sighs*] Oh, no—not that—not the heroics. You can't forgive me, can you, for being an objector!

CLIFFORD. No, it's not being an objector that infuriates me. If you had been shot for your beliefs, that would have been something. It's not your beliefs—it's you. Missing all the fun, David, the death, the fear, the hate, the pain, the legs, the arms. The fun, David, missing all the fun, and sitting here safe and smug—no pain, no fear, no answers, no questions—the nothingness of it! You're missing the party, the lanterns, fairy-lights, the laughter and the blood.

DAVID. [*quietly*] Clifford, you should have been an actor.

CLIFFORD. [*quietly*] That's right, David, my leg is strapped up behind me. Now we're back in the dressing room I needn't pretend anymore.

[*Clifford lifts his trouser leg*]

DAVID. Clifford! What do you think it's like here, alone, safe, as you say, with only a battalion of thoughts to struggle with . . . my personal war against doubt, fear, shame, hopelessness and confusion.

CLIFFORD. Then you're not happy?

DAVID. Dear God! Not that I would be any good in a war. I'd be hopeless. I suppose I could have been a stretcher-bearer or something. Anyway, I'm out of it. I hate it all. But being out of it can be worse than being in the thick of it. And with your leg—or lack of it—well, I don't feel sorry for you [*shouting*] I envy you. I envy you your pain, your wound, your rotten badge of courage.

CLIFFORD. Courage? Courage! I screamed like blue murder. I howled and hollered until one of your stretcher-bearer types collected me. I was terrified, angry and bewildered—like a child.

137

DAVID. [*quietly*] Thank you, Clifford, thank you. I know what you say is not true, but I thank you.

CLIFFORD. But it *is* true. Listen, I didn't cut my own leg off. It was blown off. It was nothing to do with me. I happened to be in the way of a passing piece of metal. You at least made your own bed of nails. You're the hero. You and you alone created your own unhappiness. Mine was, so to speak, thrust upon me.

DAVID. But I am safe, Clifford, you're right—I'm safe.

CLIFFORD. [*quietly*] Safe to suffer.

DAVID. Yes, that about sums it up.

CLIFFORD. Would you join the war, now, if you could?

DAVID. No. But I'm not happy, Clifford.

CLIFFORD. I suppose that remark is meant to satisfy me.

DAVID. Do what you like with it.

CLIFFORD. Let's forget it. Let's forget this leg. You're my brother, David. I admire you; I always have. My prowess at sport, my fame as a womanizer, my rapid rise in the army, these were all arranged by me to put you down. I deserve the loss of this leg. Yet I still used this accident to put you down.

DAVID. I admired you so much. I knew I couldn't compete. So I walked away from everything.

CLIFFORD. [*after silence*] Yes, I will have that whisky you offered me.

DAVID. Oh, sorry, David, I'll get it.

Clifford

This character is perhaps a mixture of fear and of daring. The sounds of these two words we can bring into the spoken tone of the character. To tune in, the actor could speak the word 'fear', sinking into the sound. He could also perhaps feel the gesture of

138

his mouth as he says the word 'fear'. Then speak 'dare', feeling the nature of the sounds in this word and also the mouth gesture. With these two words he may be able to tune in to something of the nature of the Clifford character. These two words are chosen as illustration; the actor can find his own.

Then, perhaps using the following phrases, he can get closer to the character and also feel the dynamic of his speech. The actor creates his own sentence for the character he plays but here is an illustration for Clifford.

'Where am I? You don't frighten me! Come and get me! If you dare.'

David

Again we have the word 'fear', but add to it the word 'peace'. The mixture of the two words and their sounds may bring the actor to a voice that is correct for the David character.

The phrases could be as follows:

'Please, let no one find me. Leave me in peace. Let this silence go on for ever. For God's sake, leave me alone.'

We begin performing these two characters as they appear from the words they speak in the script. This gives us an idea of what they are like. We may not be like them; we may disagree with them and dislike their attitudes. But they are familiar enough for us to imitate and portray them.

Having rehearsed the part of Clifford, try to recall the voice used and the general attitude of the gestures. Start with the actor's talent for imitation, then begin to understand the man. Survey your performance and find the essence of his speech and, strange as it may seem, try and bring it into a form of song. Follow this with a study of his mannerisms and bring them into dance.

Having acted out Clifford, begin to copy what you have done. In a way, withdraw yourself from the character, letting him move freely on his own and speaking in his own manner. This is not unlike the sensation we get when, having practised riding a bike

139

with someone holding the saddle, they let go. In this case, you let your character go and he begins to ride on his own. We could describe this as copying what we had created in manner and voice. The copying does not diminish the reality of the character, but it does release it from yourself.

Surveying the activity of the character in this way allows us to describe in movement and speech the essence of Clifford.

In a kind of mime dance, describe in movement the jerky counter-tension of a restrained extrovert: angry, thrusting gestures; a rhythmic dance with elbows and knees, mixed with a weary floating, as though exhausted and confused; then again angry, confused and striking out. Expand this in space, which always increases the challenge of finding the essence of a character. The more expansive the movement the more characteristically accurate it has to be. When we dance the gesture we are only slightly expanding body language, but it is an attempt to visualize the dynamics of the true gesture which lies behind the matchstick man we call ourselves. The actor can speak an invisible language so powerfully that the spectator and listener receives impressions far beyond body language, which is merely a kind of code to guide the spectator in the way the actor wishes.

By applying exactly the same principle to the speaking, the actor may also discover, on contemplating his performance, Clifford's 'melody' or 'song'. Maybe it is an unattractive song but nevertheless it is a flow of sound which is an intimate part of his character. As you recall what you did during rehearsals and hear again your own voice, you may notice a certain challenging, hectoring quality in the speaking. From this a word may arise in your inward listening, for instance the word 'dare'. You may then consider this word to be your key for the mood of his music, so you may find 'dare' absolutely the essence of this man Clifford. Divide the sound and you have the consonant 'd' and the mixed vowel of 'ae' as in 'dare'. With these two sounds you may colour the delivery of the line so that behind your character's voice and manner lie two tones which provide a backing to your character, which you may consider as a true sound picture of this man's soul. This quality may not be present at the forefront of your playing but will be there to lead the audience into the mysterious realm that exists behind our appearance. It would be a beginning.

Finally, one may find a phrase which, in manner of delivery and in the sense, conveys the thinking of this man, for instance: 'Where am I?' or 'You don't frighten me!' or 'Come and get me if you dare!' Apply the same thinking to David.

It is also a place, very like Craig's scenery, which is not always screens and rostra but intimate rooms and corridors which retain a mysterious quality in their design. So much of what we see in theatre and on our screens is dramatic, but that is only part of the craft used by the actor to take us towards drama. One of the first steps is for the actor to move more consciously into the realm of atmosphere and mood, extending his art beyond the dramatic and the familiar that we know as naturalism.

What we have discussed can also be applied to the next scene. Start with what we understand as straightforward acting, and then repeat the scene but trying to apply the ideas set down at the very end.

THE MOTHER-IN-LAW

MOTHER-IN-LAW. Oh, come in, dear. How nice of you to spare the time for a visit. I thought it would be an opportunity, now the men have gone out, for both of us to have a nice, cosy chat.

STELLA. Why do we need a cosy chat?

MOTHER. Well, I thought it would be nice.

STELLA. I'm sorry, Mrs James, but I'm not very good at such things.

MOTHER. [*laughing*] Oh, you don't have to be good at chats, leave that to me. Now, do sit down, dear. Standing like that makes you look awkward.

STELLA. I really don't see . . . Oh, all right.

MOTHER. Now, we both love John, and so in a way we both have to learn to share him.

STELLA. Mrs James, that isn't quite the case.

MOTHER. It's very much the case. That's why I wish to contribute to the happiness of your marriage.

STELLA. There's very little you can do.

MOTHER. Oh no, you're so wrong.

STELLA. [*standing*] Mrs James, John and I are something new. Our being together makes a new situation, to which the old situation of mother and son cannot contribute.

MOTHER. You're wrong, Stella. The old situation, as you call it, can never fade. That will always be there.

STELLA. Oh no. I can't bear it. Not already. Not before we're even married. I can't battle with it.

MOTHER. You must battle with it, as you so charmingly describe mother love. You have to reckon with me.

STELLA. It's just not fair.

MOTHER. Stella, do sit down. We must try and remain friends, for we have a long journey to make together. . .

[*Stella is silent*]

MOTHER. [*continues quietly*] . . . and the sooner you accept that, the better for all of us—for John, for me and, of course, for yourself.

[*Stella remains silent*]

MOTHER. Don't you agree, Stella? Stella, you must answer me when I talk to you.

STELLA. Love is a destructive thing.

MOTHER. Now, what does that mean?

STELLA. What I said. You're destroying my love for John.

MOTHER. Oh Stella, I wouldn't want to do that. But it is important that we understand each other.

STELLA. Is it? Do we have to? It would be best if John and I went away—forever.

MOTHER. If you did such a thing—I would find you both—

STELLA. Oh yes. You have little else to do. That would be a kind of play therapy for you—a treasure hunt.

MOTHER. I think you've said enough now. Your hate is hurting. I only hope you confine your venom to myself. I would be happy to suffer, as long as I could protect John from you.

STELLA. [*after a silence*] There is an old Japanese saying: 'He who raises his voice has lost the argument'. I must remember that. I must learn to handle this situation differently. Would you get me some tea, please.

MOTHER. Certainly, my dear [*stares are her for some time*]. I'll get it.

Mother

Again the word 'fear' comes to mind, perhaps with the dynamic word 'get'. This blend of sounds may find us a voice for the Mother. Her phrases could be:

> 'Come out, wherever you are! I know you're there!
> Come out or I'll come and get you! Get you my girl!'

Stella

Again we have 'fear', but added to this word are the sounds that make the word 'brave'. Again, as with the Mother, the performers can become conscious of the mouth when they say these words which may also lead them to finding the expressions for these two characters. Her phrases could be:

> 'I feel she is watching me! I know she is. I will try not to be afraid. I will be brave!'

Childhood

The actor or actress as a child is not always the most charming of children in the kindergarten. They often seem occupied with their own thoughts which they suddenly demonstrate with enormous energy, shouting and jumping about, absolutely stimulated by inner pictures, which they bring to the surface. Climbing under chairs to repair cars, they will suddenly be overtaken with an idea, which the other children cannot understand, and with great effort they will try to share their imagery, which proves far beyond their ability to explain or demonstrate. Sometimes they can become leaders, their imagination wilder than the others, and suddenly the whole class is chasing about, bewildering both themselves and the teacher. The young actor, however, well in charge of his own imagery, is frustrated that he cannot express it and make it appear.

Where the normal child will slide down the play structure provided, our actor will fling himself down headlong, picturing that he is falling from the highest mountain in the world, the short slide more than adequate for his mind to feed on. The next time he slides down, he may 'die', lying at the foot of the slide, lost in his own sense of dying. Or, if not quite 'dead', he may pick himself up slowly and limp away. This may alarm the teacher but, with a shout, he will shake his leg to show that he is not hurt at all. It is at this stage that the negative side of his acting may begin to show, for when he appeared dead he may have become aware that others, for one moment, were held spellbound. It dawns upon this little character that he can now share with them his experiences, so he begins to create laughter or anxiety, and even alarm or anger in others. Although he is accused of 'showing off', somewhere he

144

has a feeling that what he experiences he can project and share with others.

So a dramatic circle is formed, that began out of his own imagination, was transferred by his actions to stimulate the imagination of others and which in turn stimulates him to greater efforts. This social circle of fantasy can show itself in the design of old variety theatres, when they were almost a complete circle. The actor is born with this talent of transferring the imagination immediately into actions and sound. Others may paint, write or create music but the actor's medium is human behaviour. He can either show us all the familiar patterns of behaviour or reveal to us through his art a more encouraging picture of the complete human being.

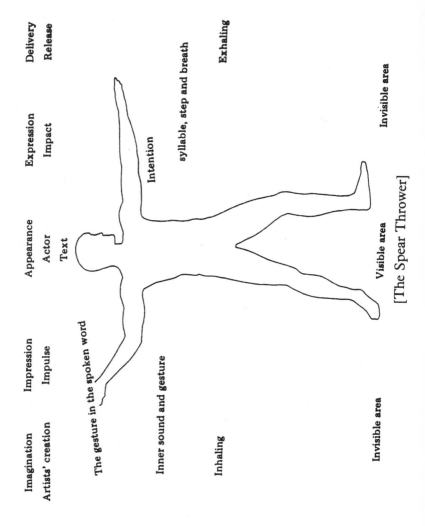

Imagination   Impression   Appearance   Expression   Delivery

Artists' creation   Impulse   Actor   Impact   Release

Text

The gesture in the spoken word

Intention

Inner sound and gesture

syllable, step and breath

Inhaling   Exhaling

Invisible area   Visible area   Invisible area

[The Spear Thrower]

146

Epilogue

In conclusion I must add a confession, which is that behind these thoughts on theatre there lies a belief. The belief, which is probably obvious by now, is that the thoughts and feelings, gestures and speaking in drama should approach the actor from another world, an invisible realm.

The drama at first exists, as it were, on the imaginary heights of a Mount Fuji or the slopes of Olympus. From this rarified atmosphere the artist calls the drama into action, into appearance. He invites the qualities which make up his art to take part in his activity. In Sophocles' *Antigone*, the Chorus cry: 'Come down the slopes of Parnassus, come rise from the surging sea, bring healing harmony with your rhythm of sound and dance.'

Hence the dramatic action is not the performer's property alone; it does not solely rely on his creative energy and skill of interpretation. He should feel that the drama speaks through his technique of gesture and speech, and not let his voice and manner bar the way to inspiration but instead evoke it.

The actor's materials ought to be his own sensitivity towards sound and gesture and his ability to allow an enhanced display of human behaviour to be expressed through his actions. These actions then expand into the whole body of the theatre and live in the audience. That is the actor's contribution.

Bibliography

Brook, Peter, *The Shifting Point*: Forty Years of Theatrical Exploration 1946-87 (Methuen, 1988).

Cotterill, H.B., *Homer's Odyssey* (Harrap, 1924).

Craig, Edward Gordon, *On the Art of the Theatre* (Heinemann, 1911).

Faulkner, Jones, D.E., *The English Spirit* (Rudolf Steiner Press).

Harvey, Paul Sir, *The Oxford Companion to Classical Literature* (Oxford University Press, 1990).

Harwood, Cecil, *Shakespeare's Prophetic Mind* (Rudolf Steiner Press, 1964).

Harwood, Cecil, *Eurythmy and the Impulse of Dance* (Rudolf Steiner Press, 1974).

Harwood, Ronald, *All the World's a Stage* (Methuen, 1984).

Josephs, B.L., *Elizabethan Acting* (Oxford University Press, 1951).

Patterson, Michael, *The Revolution in German Theatre 1900-1933* (Routledge & Kegan Paul, 1981).

Prudhoe, John, *The Theatre of Goethe and Schiller* (Basil Blackwell, Oxford 1973).

Stanislavsky, Konstantin, *My Life in Art* (Methuen, 1980).

Steiner, Rudolf & Marie, *Creative Speech: The Nature of Speech Formation* (Rudolf Steiner Press, 1978).

Steiner, Rudolf, *Eurythmy as Visible Speech* (Rudolf Steiner Press, 1984).

Steiner, Rudolf, *Speech and Drama* (Rudolf Steiner Press, 1959).